Make Acting Work

CHRYS SALT

Methuen Drama

Published by Methuen Drama

10 9 8 7 6 5 4 3 2

First published in Great Britain in 1997 by
Bloomsbury Publishing Plc
This revised and updated edition published in 2001 by
Methuen Publishing Limited

A CIP catalogue record for this book is available from the British Library

ISBN 978 0 413 76140 8

Typeset by Deltatype, Birkenhead, Merseyside

Printed and bound in Great Britain by

CPI Antony Rowe, Chippenham and Eastbourne

This book is dedicated to all my friends and colleagues in the industry, but most particularly to my indefatigable students from whom I learn so much.

Contents

Acknowledgements

This book could not have been written without the help of friends and colleagues in the profession. I am very grateful to them for their stories, wisdom, insights and information, which have been shared with characteristic kindness. Thanks are due to Bill Homewood, the late John Bishop, Betty Roe, Valerie Colgan, T. P. McKenna, Dinsdale Landen, Tim Pigott-Smith, Richard Pasco, David Quilter, Brian Galloway, Peter Wynne-Willson, Alan Franks, Robert Hitchmough, Nina Finburgh, Leonard Lewis, David Benedictus, Elizabeth Mansfield, Edward Hardwicke, John Tydeman, Janet Whitaker, Cherry Cookson, Annette Badland, David Hatton, Richard Hodder, Jack Shepherd, Oscar Watson, Robin Browne, Don Warrington, David Schofield, Lally Schofield, Souad Faress, Robert Jezek, Fiona Terry, 'Morgan' Gordon, Ellis Jones, Angela Pleasence, the late Carl Forgione, Jude Kelly, Kay Magson, Julie Fernandez, John Harrison, Colin Pinney, Kathy Clancy, Patricia Maynard, Carolyn Lucas, Karin Fernald, Pam Merrick, Nigel Seale, Jan Younger, Martin Brown, Peter Finch, Lydia Martin, Tim Block, Doreen Jones, Graham Devlin, Lyndall Goodman, Jennifer Jaffrey, Saeed Jaffrey, Bill McClean, Suzanne Alvarez, Derek Partridge, Sandra Tallent, Liz England, Penny Macdonald, Geraldine Collinge, Clive Panto, Ian Liddiard (JVC), David Timson, Jeff Capel, Carrie Dunton, Chrissie Glover, David Stonier (the London Fire Brigade), David Easton (the London Fire Brigade Press Office), Cliff Faulkner (the National Fire Service Training College), Mark Hampshire (Greater Manchester Fire Brigade), the City Police Video Unit, Vince Turnbull (the Murder Squad), Andrew Baguley (Roleplays for Training), Sharon Springall (the National Film and Television School), Chris Elwell (Central

School of Speech and Drama), Karen Rose (BBC Radio Auditions), Mark Stephens, Mark Wing Davey, Ian Pettit (the Actors Centre), the staff at the Offstage Theatre and Film Bookshop, Peter Hall (photographer), Mo Heard (formerly of MOMI), Sally Littlefair (the National Trust), Graham Farmelo and Colin Uttley (the Science Museum), John Fletcher, Simon Gregory, Joanna Aitken and Stephen Chase (Rhubarb), Bob Baker, Ron O'Brien, Andrew Manson, Frank Scantori, Vaune Craig Raymond, Hariet Lake, Elle Lewis, Bill Thomas, Bernard Shaw, Hugh Galloway, Rachael Rena, Diana Brookes, Shane Collins, Ray Newe, Tony Rex, Gareth Hunt, Sue Radford, James Brook and Stephen Ellery.

It is a pleasure to record particular thanks to Mark Stephens and the ever-helpful staff at the Actors Centre, and to my husband, Richard Macfarlane, for his understanding and support.

I am aware of the huge contribution talented women make to the industry and hope they will forgive the inevitable use of the term 'actor' to represent both actors and actresses in this book and use of the pronooun 'he' when speaking generally of actors, agents, producers, directors and casting directors.

Introduction

Actors may succeed by virtue of luck, beauty or sheer bloody talent, but most will have to learn to handle long periods of unemployment or struggle to build a career around alternative ways of earning a crust. You learn to dread the inevitable question: 'And what do you do?' (This after it has been vouchsafed that your interrogator is a nuclear physicist working on vital government research.) 'I'm an actor,' you reply, desperately trying to catch hold of the vanishing mouse-tail of your identity. 'Ah.' The eyes fill with something akin to pity. 'Resting?' (Why do they always assume you must be resting?) 'Well, no, actually, I've just finished working with Mike Leigh and I'm off to Malaga tomorrow for Barclaycard.' (Money *and* art!) Well, that's what you'd like to say. Trying to explain the thrills and spills of working at McDonald's is a bit of a conversation stopper, isn't it? Doubtful if our friend will be interested in the conundrum of how you wangle time off from the chip vat to attend an audition for a fringe show above a pub in Walthamstow, which will pay you in shoe-buttons (if you're lucky) and ensure exclusion from your bank manager's Christmas card list for the next decade. So why do we do it?

On a visit to America with the National Theatre in 1970, Sir Laurence Olivier shocked his audience by saying, 'It does seem sometimes that acting is hardly the occupation for an adult. False noses, lots of make-up and gum on my face. I can't stand it any more. But without it, I would die, I suppose.'

Acting is, of course, a vocation. No one in their right mind would sacrifice all other career options in order to do it if it weren't. At its best, it is a craft as intricate and complex as the work of a master carpenter; an art that uses as its medium the raw materials of the human soul. It can illuminate the dark corners of our shared experience. It can make us laugh. It can make us cry. The actor is an explorer across the uncharted continents of the human psyche; a chronicler, an observer, a transmitter, an entertainer, a weaver of fantasies, a clown, a magician, a soothsayer, an inhabiter of skins. At best, like Gaugin's huge *Testament Canvas*, theatre asks the questions at the root of things, 'Who are we? Where do we come from? Where are we going?' Hardly surprising we should want to be part of it!

Sadly, at worst, it is a jobbing sort of business. A cobbling together of snippets of work. A couple of lines in a sitcom here, a voice-over there. A confidence-sapping, pick-yourself-up-and-dust-yourself-down affair offering little glitz and glamour, and few financial rewards. Not what you'd been led to expect when giving your definitive Lady M at the Academy!

Perhaps you have just completed your drama-school training or university degree? Maybe you are returning to an acting career after bringing up your children, want to translate your experience as an amateur into a professional career or are seeking to make the transition from one branch of the profession to another? From dance to drama maybe? Perhaps your career is not going as well as you'd hoped.

Whether you are just starting out or are already a working actor, you not unnaturally dream of being Ralph Fiennes, Julia Roberts, Jude Law or Julie Walters. The rewards at the top of the tree seem huge. Fame, fortune, glamour – the opportunity to play great roles and take control of your creative destiny. (Interesting that the word 'fan' comes from the Latin *'fanaticus'* – somebody inspired to frenzy by devotion to a deity.) You are full of hope and ambition. You are learning your craft and are eager to build on those early foundations. If you were lucky enough to go to drama school you may have been spotted by a good agent in your end-of-year production and been taken on. This is a good start. Almost certainly you had the opportunity to cut your teeth on some decent parts in student productions before finding yourself out in the cold world looking for work.

In those solitary periods of unemployment the prospect of 'giving your Ophelia' – even at a minor Rep – seems remote. That screen test is elusive. You are one of thousands of talented thespians in the dole queue, competing for a limited number of jobs in the marketplace. You may well be able to knock spots off Alan Rickman, given half a chance, but you can't even get an audition to say 'Dinner is served' at Little Outofwork-on-Sea. A sickening realisation is beginning to nest in your heart, that without divine intervention, you may well have a longer and more intimate relationship than you would wish with a double cheeseburger.

Obvious though it may seem, being a professional actor means *working* in the profession. It means being *paid* for what you do. It requires hard work, commitment and dedication in a world where talent does not always prevail or even brilliance guarantee success.

Since writing the first edition of this book, much has changed. Computer technology dispatches actors' CVs, photographs, show-reels and demo-tapes across continents. Casting personnel in America can download your details and hear you move and speak. Casting information pops up as text messages on your mobile phone or is delivered in seconds by e-mail or accessed in Honolulu via the World Wide Web. Agenting services are available via the Internet. CVs and casting information can be published and altered at the click of a button. Casting personnel and artists can search quickly and specifically for what they want. Casting is literally expanding its 'net'.

> *When I was working at the Royal Court, someone was asked to go and see Zeffirelli. His agent said, 'Zeffirelli wants to see you; you've got the part but you've got to get to Rome as he just wants to have a look at you.' He said, 'Tomorrow you'll be picked up at home and taken to the airport in a Roller, and you'll fly first class to Rome and you'll see Zeffirelli.' He thought,* Oh my God, my career's going to change. *He was put on a first-class flight to Rome. He was picked up, brought to this big house and taken to the room where Zeffirelli was working. He knocks on the door and Zeffirelli looks up and sees him and says 'No' and continues working. Back on the plane, back in the Roller, back home. All that for 'no'!*

Gareth Hunt (actor)

Zeffirelli didn't have access to modern technology – no computer, web address, mobile phone or pager. Think of the time and money that would have been saved if he had!

The days are gone when all an actor had to do was wait for his agent to ring. Increasingly, actors need other skills as well.

If you are to survive and prosper in this difficult marketplace – with or without an agent – it is clear you need some serious strategies to secure employment. You need strategies for sustaining confidence, accessing information, defining what you have to sell and tailoring your dreams to the marketplace – strategies, in short, for getting work. This book aims to provide them.

I was making my first job application right at the beginning of my career when I came across an advertisement in The Stage *which read, 'Wanted. Young actor immediately. Prepared to do anything.' I was eighteen and had just left the RAF. I dispatched a telegram from Brighton staight away saying 'Young actor. Stop. Arriving immediately. Stop. Prepared to do anything. Stop.' Then set out at once to hitchhike to Worcester. I arrived six hours later, made my way round to the stage door where I found the stage doorman chain-smoking in his cubicle. 'Good evening, sir,' I said, 'I sent a telegram this morning ... I am a young actor prepared to do anything.' He fixed me with a beady eye, rummaged in his in-tray, picked up my telegram, tore it up, threw it in the bin and said, 'F—off!' That was the only exchange between us. So I turned round and hitchhiked all the way back to Brighton, ruefully remembering the legend in one of my old school reports. 'Misplaced optimism will get Landen nowhere!'*

Dinsdale Landen (actor)

1 A Brand Image

The Casting Process

When I first started out as a performer at the Birmingham Repertory Theatre I played everything from a fairy to an aged crone. One month I was wearing ringlets, the next I was sword-fighting in a codpiece! However talented and versatile you are, there are precious few opportunities to do that these days. It's a buyer's market. Things have changed beyond recognition.

Back in the 1950s and 1960s plays in regional theatres would be cast from a permanent company of actors who would be hired for at least a season. John Harrison, former Artistic Director of several prominent regional Reps (now Director Emeritus of the West Yorkshire Playhouse) used to audition once, or at most twice, a year. There was no question of typecasting. Plays were inevitably 'through-cast' and actors would appear in most plays in the season – rehearsing in the daytime, playing at night. Actors were cast because they were 'least wrong' rather than 'most right'. Everybody's skills were stretched and challenged. Learning from their peers enriched young actors' work. It was a training ground which gave British theatre one of the richest skill bases in the world. We have good reason to fear for it now.

Today, theatre companies no longer 'through-cast', with a few notable exceptions like the Royal Shakespeare Company and Pitlochry. Actors are generally cast in one-off parts, with precious few opportunities to learn on the job. Guest directors import their own people. (Actors with families, mortgages and responsibilities can't afford to spend months in the provinces either, especially now the celluloid media offer such rich pickings.) Nor are the celluloid media well known for taking wild imaginative leaps when it comes to casting. A friend who works regularly in television complained to me recently, 'I joined this profession to use my skills to transform and communicate. Now all I'm ever asked to do is play myself.'

However much you dislike it, it would be foolish and counter-productive to shut your eyes to the reality of the current marketplace. In all kinds of media – television, the cinema, literature, magazines, hoardings – a stereotypical world continues to be created with all the images that Western culture has been peddling at us for centuries in myth, literature, art and fairy tales. From Greek and Roman times it has reinforced the view that the 'body beautiful' is an ideal and that those with physical imperfections are seen as objects of fear and fun – Richard III, Dr Strangelove, Captain Hook, Freddie in *Elm Street*, etc. As a result, today's celluloid entertainment (the theatre too to some extent) has a tendency to cast by appearances and ones that reinforce deeply rooted perceptions. It is what the great actor Nabil Shaban calls 'body fascism' – the belief that 'physical beauty takes you closer to goodness and the converse takes you further away'. We all consciously or unconsciously fall prey to this and casting directors are no less susceptible than the rest of us. Our audiences especially are not immune.

When you first walk through the casting director's door, the 'perfume' of your personality combined with your physical appear-ance creates an immediate first impression that is difficult to dislodge. If you look like Daniel Day Lewis you won't get cast as Quasimodo (unless, of course, you are fortunate enough to *be* Daniel Day Lewis, who gets cast as everything!). How many casting directors think of an actor's capabilities as a performer before his physical appearance? Yet everybody knows that Fiona Shaw can play Richard III, Annette Badland can play Titania, Nabil Shaban can play Volpone and the Asian actress Souad Faress can play Lady Capulet (with a white Juliet) – and be marvellous. When performances succeed, conventional 'miscasting' often goes by without comment. ('To miscast is to cast most well,' said Peter Brook.) It is hard to see why casting personnel are so resistant to making choices purely on the basis of talent when innovative choices invariably reward them with stimulating and surprising work. Nevertheless, it seems to be the exception rather than the rule. As a result, actors get few opportunities to demonstrate their versatility.

Unless you have a brilliant agent who fights to get you seen for parts not specifically written for Asians, it is almost impossible. There are only a handful of casting directors who think of the actor first and not the face.

Souad Faress (actor)

I know I'm good at my job but what you have to prove first to a producer is that it's OK to employ a disabled person. It means that my capabilities as a performer are secondary to my wheelchair. Sometimes I sit down on the settee of an evening after a hard day and think, 'Damn ... maybe I'll just give it all up ...' But I never will because I love it too much. I'm a fighter. It isn't a very good reflection on society, is it? It's the black issue, the gay issue; it's the disabled issue, it's the fat issue, it's the thin issue – it's the whole typecasting issue. They are missing out on so much talent!

Julie Fernandez (actor)

People use different standards when it comes to black actors. It's hard to put one's finger on it but I suspect it's because black people are still representative of something. They are not themselves. They are not simply the character. They have to be 'a type'. Every actor has to be 'a type' but I think it's exaggerated in terms of black actors. It has to do with their perceptions of what 'being black' is, as opposed to who the character is. People assume an added dimension when they are dealing with black actors. Your ability is secondary to your physicality. Of course I accept to some extent that it is true for everybody – but for black actors the difficulties are so much greater.

Don Warrington (actor)

When I was young and living in New York I didn't have an agent so I would ring several agents every day and make appointments to see them. I would carry my album of photographs and reviews from Catholic U [Drama School] summer stock in Winooski and the Shakespearean tour, and go and meet these New York agents who knew nothing about India as a country, let alone an Indian actor who acted in the English language. So these meetings were largely unsuccessful. I would do a soliloquy from Hamlet *or* Richard III *and the reply I would usually get would be, 'Oh my Gaad! That's wonderful, marvellous, almost as good as Laurence Aalivier! But there are no parts for* Indians *this year. Sorry.'*

Saeed Jaffrey (actor)

I was in my early twenties and there was a production to be mounted at Drury Lane of Hello Dolly. *My agent had put me up for the Michael Crawford part and I sang 'Younger than Springtime' from* South Pacific . . . *I'd always wanted to be that man . . . Lieutenant Cable. It was a terrifying experience. It was exactly what you would expect it to be like. A cattle market. A huge stage. A big black hole with some unidentified people down in the stalls. So I did my song, my knees like jelly, giving my all. When I got to the end there was a pause, then a female voice, an American, shouted out from the utter darkness. 'Thank you very much. We are looking for somebody a little taller . . .'*

David Schofield (actor)

My father had been cast in the lead of a big horror movie and I was called up to audition for the part of his daughter. Obviously I thought it was a foregone conclusion. The Americans thought it was a wonderfully interesting idea but concluded that 'Angela Pleasence is completely wrong to play Donald Pleasence's daughter . . .'

Angela Pleasence (actor)

Define your Product

Actors must learn to think of themselves as small businesses with a product to sell. The product is their artistry. What are those qualities that 'define' you as an artist? *Whom* do you have to sell? Success depends on the quality of your product and tailoring its individual and special qualities to the marketplace.

What is your product? What makes you unique? Ask friends. Ask relatives. Ask other actors. Ask them to be honest. How do they see you? Take a candid look at yourself in the mirror. Are you tall and thin? Short and fat? Worldly? Innocent? Weird and wacky? Sultry and seductive? Built like a barn? What are your particularities or peculiarities? What makes you distinctive and special? It's not only your looks that make you what you are. Where do you come from? Where did you go to school? What social class are you from? What are the experiences that have shaped your life? Identify those qualities that make you different and sell them for all you are worth.

> *An actor can be a virtuoso, mimic or chameleon in their range but there are certain intangible things that you can usually put your finger on – for example, class . . . The reason why those films in the 1950s really worked with Albert Finney and Tom Courtney was because they were no longer saying, 'Cor blimey, Governor . . .' There are understandings that actors have from their own lives . . . you're not a neutral vessel as an actor, you are an artist and you bring with you your history, your understanding, your moral conflicts, your own sense of humour . . . and that will feed into the way the part gets done . . . Maybe if actors were more confident of being artists – I know that's a paradox because an actor's choice as an artist is to say, 'yes' or 'no' and that's not a very businesslike position for any artist to be in – but it is important for them to think of themselves as artists and be trained to think like that so that they come in to a job to contribute – not to be directed – but to* contribute their work as an artist *and therefore to try to say 'I haven't got anything special, I haven't got the identity, I can be anything' – it's a sort of prostitution almost to want to be so devoid of personal qualities that define you as an artist.*

Jude Kelly (Artistic Director, West Yorkshire Playhouse)

Some years ago I was casting a play about the Arab–Israeli conflict. I was looking for a tall Arab girl with waist-length hair. The script required it. Imagine my surprise when, opening one submission, I found a photo of a cheery young woman with distinctly Anglo-Saxon features and a letter, which read: 'I am applying for the role of "Yasmin". I am short and fair, but very versatile.' I didn't audition her, but the story does raise a number of interesting points about the audition process and actors' desperation to find work. In my hunt for 'Yasmin' I had no problem in finding the 'real thing'. The actor I cast not only fulfilled all the physical requirements for the role, which in this case were important, but was also able to bring to it a knowledge of the background and culture that the play addressed. Her history, her family background, her understanding of the issues gave her a head start. It would have been counter-productive to consider our Anglo-Saxon friend, for all her versatility. I was of course 'typecasting' and actors complain about it all the time, but until you become famous enough to have more influence over the casting process it is a fact of life.

Jude Kelly (Artistic Director, West Yorkshire Playhouse)

When I was on the RADA Audition Panel, some people would audition who didn't get chosen but you knew would make a living in the profession. Absolutely. Without any shadow of a doubt. You wanted to say (but you couldn't) – 'Don't bother about this. Go out there. You'll get work.' Others were brilliant, but you knew they would struggle all their lives because there was no 'slot' for them . . .

Edward Hardwicke (actor)

Case Studies

Students who attend my regular class at the Actors Centre are uncompromisingly honest when it comes to defining each other's 'saleable qualities'. Family, colleagues and friends can fulfil the same useful function.

John trained as a teacher and was a late entrant to drama school. After graduating, his teaching experience led him to work with a range of Theatre in Education companies, playing everything from a cumulus cloud to a free-range hen! When the funding ran out John found himself without the usual outlet for his skills and with no clear idea of whom he had to sell, there being a conspicuous shortage of opportunities for free-range hens! Photographs portrayed him as nothing in particular – an ordinary-looking nice guy in his mid-forties. An Actors Centre group saw him rather differently. Working class! Seedy, downtrodden, smarmy! A touch of the conman! A bit of an old lag. Honesty, not tact, is the necessary hallmark of the group! John took it all very well. Armed with a suitable moustache, a fresh set of moustachioed photos and a new audition piece cobbled from an episode of *The Bill*, John set out with a much clearer idea of how to market his product – certainly for television. A couple of months later I received a postcard. His first small television part was as a used-car salesman in a well-known police series! He is now building on his experience and beginning to play a wider range of parts.

After graduating from RADA, Susi had a very successful career in the theatre before marrying and bringing up four kids. Thirty years on she decided to make a comeback, but with no idea of the parts she might play. Her days of playing Viola were sadly over, although I would love to have seen her. When she vouchsafed that she was nearly seventy, we were genuinely stunned. We were so impressed by her energy and verve. The group agreed that Susi was definitely aristocrat, not peasant. A headmistress type. A 'classical' feel. A professional with a touch of the Joyce Grenfells. She had a marvellous flair for comedy. A glamorous gran, perhaps – she radiated class and poise. Susi took it all on board. In no time at all she had replaced her photographs and a Sloanier, more upmarket Susi shone from her 10x8s. I bumped into her quite by accident a while later. She had been out of work for some time, but had stuck to her guns and been taken on by a good agent who had put her up for a series of short comedy films. The producers had wanted 'a lady, to the manor born'. A lovely part. She didn't even have to audition. She had other auditions lined up and was very optimistic about the future.

> Garry was an East End lad. Leather jacket. Brylcreemed hair. He was so hung up on 'being an actor', 'getting rid of his accent', 'never having been to drama school', that he completely undersold the warm, funny, rough-diamond, Jack-the-lad, saleable qualities that he had in abundance. The group soon put him right. Garry was a natural. Armed with the confidence to 'be himself' he went from strength to strength. The next time I saw him he was in a few episodes of *EastEnders*. Then there was a Mike Leigh film . . .

The point of these stories is clear. Casting directors need all the help they can get to make those difficult casting decisions and actors must target themselves at work *for which they are best suited*. All my Actors Centre friends had skills and talents that stretched far beyond these crude stereotypes, but by identifying a 'market niche' they were all able to get that vital foot through the door. Once your work is seen and known, you will be in a much stronger position to convince them of your range and versatility.

Here is a true, if somewhat immoral story, which makes the point.

> A young woman, fresh out of drama school, won the opportunity to audition for a part in a high-profile film. She wasn't right and didn't get it. Keen and ambitious, she set about finding out exactly what the director wanted. She changed her name, changed her accent, changed her image to fit the bill and applied to audition again with a fresh set of photos and a new identity. This time it was a different story. The director was delighted with his 'find'. It was only after she had been filming for a few days that the full extent of her duplicity became known and was splashed across the pages of the tabloid press. She had made herself very unpopular, but her contract was signed and it was too late for anyone to do anything about it.

While not advocating such extreme measures, actors clearly do need to employ legitimate strategies to survive and flourish in an increasingly difficult marketplace. Work breeds work. When opportunities to practise your craft are so few and far between, it makes sense to grab every one that comes along. You need to learn on the job. All experience is grist to the mill. You only have to switch on your television to conclude that it's the actor who has carved that specific market niche for himself who continues to work. Why do some actors always play 'heavies'? Why are some rarely seen out of uniform? Why does Sean Bean never get cast as an aristocrat? (I'm sure he would be wonderful.) How do casting directors see you? Let's see what can be done to maximise your prospects.

2 A Marketing Package

Once you have a clear idea of the image you want to promote, you will need to develop a marketing package in order to sell your product effectively.

You will need headed paper, compliment slips, business cards and postcards, a clear CV and a good set of photographs. You will also need a demo-tape if you are seeking voice work and a showreel for work on screen.

A standard package will consist of a CV, a photograph, a brief letter and a large self-addressed envelope. Every package you send out must reflect who you are and the image you are trying to sell.

Your CV

If you haven't worked for a director before, often the first introduction will be your CV and photograph. Make sure your CV is a professional and 'selling' document.

We live in a high-tech age. Most actors possess or have access to computers. If not, your local print shop will design and produce your CV at modest cost.

There is an excellent selection of coloured and textured papers available. Choose one you feel 'fits' your personality. Bear in mind that dark, rich colours don't fax too well.

Rationalise colour and typefaces on all your stationary. You might consider a logo to reinforce your image. (One actor whose surname is Bearfoot devised a delightful freehand footprint for his package. Very memorable.) Be careful, though – don't make it too tricksy.

Borders can look good. Contrasting colours are effective. Keep your CV short. One side of A4 is enough, although CVs can come in many shapes and formats. Stapled pages often separate during the casting process.

Present your credits clearly. Directors don't have time to 'unpick' it.

Keep your CV 'on disc' so you can update it when necessary or 'tailor' it to suit the job you are applying for.

Content

Your name – Make it Big and Bold and Memorable. You want the director to remember you. Choose a typeface that suits you. (Remember – your name is not Curriculum Vitae!) The Letraset catalogue or a friendly printer will tell you all you need to know about typefaces.

Your address and telephone number (plus ansaphone, fax, e-mail, mobile and pager numbers if you have them) – Nobody in the theatre works from nine until five. It's vital you can be contacted at any time of the day or night. (Make a habit of calling in to your ansaphone once a day if you are away from home.)

If your agent (see page 45) is sending out your CV on his own headed paper, which is the normal procedure, try to ensure that his name and logo do not dwarf yours. Make sure he consults you about the content and layout. After attending my course, an actor with a rich CV took the reconstituted model to her high-flying agent, who had hitherto insisted on a certain format. After studying the revised format he apologised, agreed it was a significant improvement and undertook to send it out on her behalf in future! If you don't have an agent, at least you don't have that problem.

Your training – If you have been to one of the recognised and reputable drama schools or done a related degree at university, all well and good. Put it on your CV. If not, let your credits do the talking. Indications of ongoing training will always impress and in my view are essential. If you are studying mime, training at the Actors Centre, learning Serbo-Croat or doing a diploma in stage combat, let it be known.

Your personal details – Your photograph will tell a director much of what he needs to know about your appearance, but additional information about height, weight or colouring – particularly if it is out of the ordinary – can be very helpful. A thin face can often belie a portlier body. Short people can often look 6ft 2ins from the chest up. Redheads can look brunette. Some actors include their hat size and inside leg measurement. It's not necessary. The wardrobe mistress will want these details *after* you have landed the part!

Your Equity number (see chapter 8) – While the law has changed with regard to membership of a trades union, your Equity number, if you have one, will reassure employers that you have at least the bare minimum of experience to achieve union membership.

Your *Spotlight* number – This enables a director to see another image or find you in the *Spotlight* directory (see chapter 3) if your photograph has become detached from your CV.

Your playing age – An actor's CV differs from standard CVs in this respect. Don't put your real age or date of birth – that only pigeon-holes you in a director's mind. Make sure you have a clear idea of the age range you can play. Perhaps you are twenty-four but can play teenagers. Maybe you are in your fifties but haven't worn too well. Take a long, hard look at yourself. Ask strangers how old they think you are. 'I see from your CV that you are twenty-eight. What a pity. I loved your audition but we were looking for someone in their early thirties . . .' Let them make their own assessment within reasonable parameters.

Your credits – These should be set out clearly and be easy to read. Arrange them under headings: Theatre, Television, Film, Commercials, Sound. If you have played modest parts with well-known directors or in the West End, you can vary the type size to draw attention to the more impressive aspects. If you have worked with a director more than once, make it clear. There must be some good reason why they asked you back!

It is not necessary to present your credits in chronological order. If you have played Ophelia in *Hamlet* to 'Somebody-Awfully-Famous' it makes sense not to bury it halfway down just because you did pantomime in Farnham more recently. Some casting directors, like Kay Magson at the West Yorkshire Playhouse, like to see dates. There is no need to be terribly specific. '1984–6 Rep, including . . .' will probably do the trick if things look thin. If you have taken time out to have a baby or bike around the world it might be as well to mention it to explain the gaps. However tempting it might be to 'enhance' your credits, or even invent new ones, it's not to be recommended.

> *I was auditioning for the part of Feste in* Twelfth Night *at the Young Vic. I'd read well, improvised well, knew the text backwards and was all but discussing the fee before I left via the stage door. Then the director called me back: 'Before you go,' he said, 'perhaps we'd better just hear you play the mandolin . . .' My agent had told a whopper and there was no getting out of this one!*
>
> Simon Gregory (actor)

Your skills – Think carefully. Most people have more skills than they realise. If you can swim, handle a canoe, scuba-dive, play a recorder, have a certificate in stage combat, can horse-ride or pole-vault seven buses, make sure it features on your CV. The director will want to know. Can you sing? Are you trained? Can you hold a tune or are you a strong soprano with a range between low A and top C? Can you dance or are you just a 'good mover'? What kind of dance? Jazz? Tap? Lindy hop? A performer will often gain the edge because of particular skills over and above the ability to act. I once had to cast the part of a cellist who could juggle – not, I hasten to add, at the same time. Any working director or casting director will receive literally thousands of CVs a year. If you have done something particularly interesting like mounted your own show, learned to play the accordion or ridden a unicycle over a vat of boiling marmalade, make sure it's included. It might just be the fascinating detail that catches the eye and makes the difference between being a contender or on the 'reject' pile.

> *I think it's quite a good idea to add something unlikely and improbable to your list of interests or skills. It's a talking point. A lot of auditions are an embarrassment on both sides while you try to find some common ground. For instance, when I went up to Channel 4 to rubber-stamp my appointment as Commissioning Editor for Drama*

Series, I sat next to Edmund Dell, the ex-Postmaster General, who was on the Board. 'I've been looking at your CV,' he said, '... very interesting things you've got up to. What's this? Special interest in cheese ... That's very unusual.' My CV actually said 'chess', but I managed to wax lyrical about cheese for quite some time!

David Benedictus (actor and novelist)

Accents – Make sure any accent you claim is native or accurate. Indicate you have a 'good ear' if you can pick up accents quickly. Most actors are good mimics and companies will often have a dialect coach to help you if you land the part. If you speak a foreign language, make sure it is included on your CV too. Indicate your level of fluency. A good working knowledge of a language will enable you to work in other countries as well.

If you ask what attracts me to a CV ... Good work. What I know to have been good work will attract me to a CV. For example, if somebody has done fifteen Ray Cooney tours I'll think, 'Well, it's unlikely that they have a desperate desire ... a desperate desire, to play Gertrude' – otherwise they would have done it, or tried to do it, or tried to make some other choices about what they did. You can only see from a CV what an actor has done and surmise why they have done it and what it is that they love about theatre. If someone writes to you and says, 'I've done fifteen Ray Cooney farces but I assure you that I've always wanted to do Shakespeare. Please, let me play the maid with four lines because I just want to be near that,' you are likely to see if that might be possible. It says something about the kind of person they are ...

Jude Kelly (Artistic Director, West Yorkshire Playhouse)

Keep your CV up to date. 'What have you been doing lately?' comes the inevitable question. 'Nora in *A Doll's House* at Salisbury Rep,' you reply proudly, groping for the reviews in your handbag. If it's not on your CV, no one will remember it at the end of a long day of auditions.

A simple, clear and effective CV might look like this:

HERMIONE JOBBING-THEATRICAL
Trained at the Royal Academy of Dramatic Art 1995–8

149 Talent Avenue
Richworth
London NW3 3NT
Tel: 020 8999 9999
Fax: 020 8888 8888
Mob: 077XXXXXX
e-mail: herjob@cs.com

Agent
Fab Management
100 Job Lane
London W1 1AA
Tel: 020 7111 1111
Fax: 020 7222 2222
e-mail: cast@demon.com

Height. 4ft 11ins
Build. Large
Hair. Titian

Playing Age. 25–35
Equity No. 7777
Spotlight No. 4444

Theatre

Big Mol	*Moll's Revenge*	Famous Theatre Co.	**Peter Hall**

Television

Clarry	*The Bill*	Granada	**Bill Bloggs**

etc. etc.

Film

Madame Rouge	*Say No*	Good Films	**Bill Bloggs**

etc. etc.

Commercials

Include Mars, Ryvita, Slumberland, Barclays Bank. (List available on request.)

Sound

Many broadcasts. Six months with BBC English Rep.

Skills

Clean Driving Licence (car and motorbike), scuba-diving (BSAC Certificate), aerobics, parachute-jumping, trained strong soprano (low A–top C), jazz dance.

Accents

Native South African. RP. Good ear. Fluent Afrikaans.

Photographs

Money is more frequently wasted on photographs than anything else. A good set of photographs is vital to an actor's armoury, yet so often they are of poor quality and don't give a clear idea of the image the actor is seeking to promote.

Choosing a photographer

Good photographers are expensive, so it is important to get value for money. (Don't be tempted to use the holiday snap of you looking happy and relaxed in Ibiza – it will look woefully inadequate beside a crisp professional shot.) Think of your investment as 'risk capital'. One little television job will pay for it 'at a stroke' but first you must get through the casting director's door. Your photographs will be with you for several years, so it's important you get it right.

Most of us would rather go to the dentist than have our photograph taken. We respond to the camera rather like a rabbit caught in the gaze of a snake. Important, then, to choose a photographer with whom you feel safe and confident; one who understands what is required of a theatrical shot. You need to know that the photographer is competent; that he will provide a relaxed and enabling environment for your session.

Most photographers get their work by word of mouth, so ask other actors whom they favour. Also look through *Contacts* and *Spotlight* (see chapter 3) to see what photographs catch your eye. Pay a few visits to photographers' studios, talk about what you want, ask to see portfolios, ask about prices and compare. Some photographers like to work in natural light, others feel a studio shot delivers a more accurate likeness, so that should also be a consideration. If you think you will feel more relaxed on a bench in your own back garden, you will need to seek out a photographer who 'has camera – will travel'.

The photograph

A really good photograph will look like you and capture the essence of your personality. No photograph can get you the job, but it can get you through the door. You are halfway there if your photo has impressed. A good photographer will spend time talking to you before the shoot, not only to make you feel more at home but to discover if there is any particular specification for the session. Do you want a good natural shot for *Spotlight* or something more specific for a particular job? Arrive at the session knowing what you want and explain it clearly. Take charge of the session. You are paying for it. You are not a piece of meat to be arranged and rearranged on a slab. Some dos and don'ts . . .

- Wear clothes in which you feel comfortable. Take a variety to the session, so you can ring the changes.
- Avoid cluttered necklines and distracting jewellery. This is not a photograph of your grandma's emeralds.
- Be conscious of the image you are trying to create and dress accordingly. If you are generally cast as bank managers and solicitors, reinforce your image with a suit. Women should be wary of too much cleavage. It will distract from your face unless you are going for specific roles for which it is appropriate.
- Try to ensure a neutral background. Dark hair can disappear into a dark background, however moody it makes you look. Conversely, fair hair against a pale background will make your photograph look very washed-out. Open-air backgrounds can reinforce your image. A slightly wind-blown shot beside a lake will make you look lyrical. A leather jacket against a brick wall will make you look butch. Be sure that these are the images you want to convey. Beware of clichés. Whatever you choose, confirm with your photographer that the background will not be fussy or distracting. You must be the star of this photograph, not the setting.
- Ask the company who does your reproductions to put your name on the bottom border. Photographs often get detached from CVs and a casting director is more likely to pass you over if your documents can't be easily reunited. One photographer told me about an enquiry he received from a casting director asking him if he could identify an actor from a physical description and the description of some distinctive earrings. The photographer's name was on the photo but not the performer's! Luckily he could. In fact,

under copyright law your photographer's name should be on your photo as well. The law is generally ignored and nobody sues, but if you are pleased with the product, ask for some stickers. You should by rights advertise the photographer on your prints too.

- Ask your photographer to print up some 6 x 4 postcards. These can be tremendously useful. They are cheaper than 10 x 8s and are effective reminders: 'Dear Peter, I'm having a wonderful time playing Tench in a revival of John Galsworthy's *Strife* ...' Postcards often hang around on people's desks for ages and are a constant reminder of your existence.

- Don't airbrush out those characterful wrinkles. A nasty pimple can go but moles, scars, birthmarks, etc. contribute to your individuality. What if Kirk Douglas had airbrushed his chin ... ?

- Make sure you have a new set of photographs taken if you have made some drastic alteration to your appearance like growing your hair or shaving your beard. If you don't, your arrival might be very disconcerting. In any case you ought to update your photographs every two or three years.

- Send 10 x 8s if you are applying for a job. My experience is that anything smaller disappears in the pile.

- Ensure you have a decent selection. Photographs play a key role in the casting process. Match the photograph as closely as you can to the casting requirement.

- Don't bother with composites (photographs with several different images on the same sheet). They generally look like Hermione Jobbing-Theatrical in a hat, Hermione J-T smoking a pipe, Hermione J-T with her hair up ... Go for a single strong image. Composites can be very confusing and they are expensive. After all, transformation comes from within!

- Don't send a colour photograph. It will make you look like a model. Black-and-white is the convention, so stick to that. It is significantly cheaper too.

- Don't go to the hairdresser and a make-up artist before your session. If you are called to a last-minute audition you will never be able to simulate the effect and your photograph will do you a disservice.

- Consult your agent before spending a fortune. He knows what he is trying to sell.
- Find a firm that does decent reproductions (repros) of your photograph. Your photographer can obviously provide you with prints but a company that specialises in repros has the technology to provide them in bulk and will be much cheaper. You can do transactions by post once you have identified a good company. Several firms advertise regularly in *The Stage* and in *Contacts*. Most companies charge around the same price, but some take more care than others. Actors generally need their repros in a hurry and for some reason never seem to complain. A wonderful photograph can be ruined by poor reproduction. You should provide the repro company with a good black-and-white 10 x 8 print for them to copy. Alternatively, some photographers will supply original negatives. Repros printed from those will be the best. Repros printed from copy negatives (made from original 10 x 8s) are more usual and almost as good. Digital prints are quicker and cheaper, but I don't think the quality is quite up to scratch. Check which method your repro company uses and ask to compare examples of their repros against originals before spending your money. Steve Luck at Image (56 Shepherds Bush Road, London w6 7PH Tel: 020 7602 1190 Fax: 020 7602 6219 www.imagephotographic.com) offers a top-notch fast and friendly service. Or there's a wonderful little firm in Penzance – Courtwood Profiles (Courtwood, Freepost TO55 Penzance, TR18 2BR Tel: 01736 365 222 Fax: 01736 36522) – which produces excellent stick-on repros (from stamp-size up) by return of post at amazingly low cost.

Finally, if you have the technology and have run out of repros you can always scan your 10 x 8s into your computer and print them out on photo-quality paper. In extremis, try a print shop with a quality colour photocopier. Both a bit more expensive, but useful options in a tight corner!

What should you expect to pay and what do you get?
At the time of writing a set of photographs costs anything between £60 and £250 excluding VAT. The length of the session will vary and

bears no relation to the quality of the product. Photographers work in different ways. At the upper end of the market your photographer might shoot two rolls of film, giving seventy-two shots to choose from. Included in the price he will let you have your contact sheets, on which he will often mark his preferences plus (say) five 10 x 8s of your own choosing. (Take some notice of your photographer's choices. He will be able to offer you an experienced and objective eye. Your partner will choose one that makes you look ravishing. Your mum will choose one for her mantelpiece.) You need a selection of crisp candid shots that look straight into the director's eye with a strong positive energy. Take your time. More often than not, the right ones will leap at you from the contact sheet. You will keep coming back to them. Extra prints (hand prints) will cost around £6. Many photographers offer special discount rates for drama students. Repros cost around £35 for fifty 10 x 8s The cost generally decreases on a sliding scale for larger orders. There will be a modest extra cost for printing your name on your photograph, which I would strongly recommend.

Portfolios

Some actors carry a small portfolio containing photographs, reviews, newspaper cuttings, shots of themselves on stage and stills from their TV and film performances. They are rarely opened but they can sometimes be useful. An established actor of my acquaintance – well known for playing slightly 'barmy' parts – convinced a director that she had a wider range by showing him the saner, more 'housewifely' shots in her portfolio.

A portfolio can be a useful prop if a director wants to know more about you. It gives you both something to talk about.

Portfolio cases are inexpensive and can be obtained from most good stationers. Occasionally they provide additional evidence about your work and your abilities, which could just tip the balance.

When I arrived at the Actors Playhouse to meet the director of the off-Broadway hit, Lorca's Blood Wedding, a rather nervous-looking lady in her early thirties met me, saying 'Gosh! But you're far too young for the part. They should've told me you're in your early twenties.' 'I'm almost thirty – and please look at these,' I said, showing my album of reviews and photographs, adding, 'And who's that with the balding head and long grey beard? That's me, ma'am, as Friar Lawrence. All over the States people not only accepted me as this old priest, they also sang my praises. Look at the reviews!' Impressed, she agreed to let me audition and said the part was the Father of the Bride. I read it and was instantly offered the part!

Saeed Jaffrey (actor)

The Letter

The letter you enclose with your CV and photograph should be no more than a short but effective explanation as to why you are applying for this particular job.

Write on headed paper that matches your CV and reinforces your 'brand image'. It won't matter if the letter is typed or handwritten, as long as your writing is legible. One or two directors I have spoken to say they prefer handwritten letters because they get some 'feel' of the applicant from them, but this is by no means a universal view. Find out the director's name and address him personally. 'Dear Sir or Madam' is alienating and suggests an unprofessional approach. Find out as much as you can about the production. Ring up and ask. PAs and secretaries can often be very helpful. If you have an agent, he or she will doubtless have received a 'cast breakdown' and will pass on any relevant information.

'Cast breakdowns' for many productions are published in the casting information sheets (see chapter 3). They give the name of the company and the director, information about auditions and venues and opening dates, and a very rough description of the characters that are being cast, i.e.:

A Midsummer Night's Dream by William Shakespeare

PRODUCTION INFORMATION

Production Company:	Bare Boards ... *and a passion*
Director:	Chrys Salt
Auditions:	From mid-June (TBA)
Rehearsal dates:	From 10 August 2001
Opening date:	2 September 2001
Venue:	The Round House, then touring

This well-known Shakespeare comedy will be set in the Caribbean and requires an all-black cast.

Oberon: Actor playing mid-thirties. Tall. Beautiful. Arrogant. Jealous. Dangerous. King of the fairies.

Titania: etc. etc.

Here is a sample letter in response to my fictional advertisement that is effective and to the point.

JONATHAN JOBBING-THEATRICAL

149 Talent Avenue	Agent
Richworth	Fab Management
London NW3 2NT	100 Job Lane
Tel: 020 8999 9999	London W1 1AA
Fax: 020 8888 8888	Tel: 020 7111 1111
	Fax: 020 7222 2222

Dear Chrys Salt,

A Midsummer Night's Dream

I understand you will be auditioning for an all-black production of *The Dream* in the next few weeks and are seeking a tall Oberon. I am Afro-Caribbean and six foot two! You will see from my CV that I played Aaron in *Titus Andronicus* on a grand tour of schools and arts centres last year, so already have experience of tackling a major Shakespearean

---

> role. That production was exceptionally well received. I enclose two of
> our reviews for your information.
>
> I am keen to learn more about your approach to the play. I do hope
> I can come in and audition for you.
>
> Yours sincerely, etc. etc.

Enclose a large, stamped, strong, self-addressed envelope for the safe
return of your photograph. Freelance theatre directors involved in
one-off productions will almost certainly not want to keep it; nor will
they have the time or money to return it. However, casting directors
for the bigger theatre companies, TV and film may well want to keep
you on file, especially if you are a 'type'. (Our tall Afro-Caribbean
applicant is a case in point.) A self-addressed envelope offers the best
chance of receiving a reply of some kind. More often than not, no one
will tell you when you haven't got the job.

Finally, make sure you devise an efficient and simple information
storage and retrieval system, so you can keep track of all that
correspondence as it accumulates.

Demo-tapes

> *To be successful in getting voice work you have to be extremely
> focused on the realities of the voice business. Unless you are 'famous'
> you are unlikely to get a voice agent. Most potential employers are
> happy to be approached directly by voice artists. Be very clear about
> what you have to offer and research specific requirements of each
> potential employer. Match your strengths to their needs, use your
> voice to sell your voice and don't hide behind the dreaded Jiffy bag.*
>
> Bernard Shaw (voice-over producer and author of
> *Voice-Overs – a Practical Guide*)

Before you can get work in the lucrative field of voice-overs (see
chapter 7) – and the competition is very, very tough – you will need
to provide yourself with a demo-tape.

A demo-tape is a compilation on a short audio cassette of an actor's voice work. It is your audition for work in this field. It is generally no more than five minutes long and should have four or five contrasting advertisements on one side and a short commentary (anything from the voice-over from a documentary to a paragraph read from a novel) on the other. Actors who work regularly in this field will have no problem in getting a demo-tape together by compiling it from existing material. Those of you hoping to make a start will need to be creative. Be encouraged. If you aren't lucky enough to have a few useful snippets from the BBC and Radio Solent to string together, you can start from scratch and create the material for yourself.

Making and marketing a demo-tape is a costly business, so if you are interested in doing this kind of work, *find some classes* or seek advice before embarking. If you are a member of Equity, the Actors Centre runs excellent voice-over workshops by seasoned practitioners. They will give you honest advice about whether you've got what it takes. If your voice is distinctive; if you can sound enthusiastic about a new lavatory cleaner; if your ear is tuned to the subtle stresses and nuances of language; if you can sight-read the telephone directory with conviction and have a stopwatch in your head, you already have a few of the qualities needed. Practise with a tape recorder at home. You'll be surprised. It's harder than you think. The best practitioners can shave a quarter of a second off a take without giving it a second thought and yet some of the most brilliant actors don't seem to have 'the knack'.

> *Most people spend their lives 'saying what they don't mean'. The voice artist has the ability to reverse this situation and 'mean what they don't say'. To achieve this one needs absolute control of the three Ps – Pitch, Pace and Pause. The hardest of these is pitch. Voices with problems in this sensitive department are said to be suffering from the increasingly common Lewinsky Syndrome – currently defined as 'going down in the wrong places'!*
>
> Bernard Shaw (voice-over producer and author of
> *Voice-Overs – a Practical Guide*)

Begin by listening carefully to the TV and commercial radio stations that run ads. This will give you an idea of the standard and style that is expected. Ads range from ones for computer dating ('you too can find love . . .') to ones for classy bedroom centres and government campaigns. Each will have a particular 'feel': hard-sell or soft-sell. The voice for a particular beauty product might be soft and silky. The voice for an effective cleaning fluid might be that of an abrasive 'shouter'.

Advertisements on buses, the Underground or in the Sunday colour supplements will give you source material to practise on. Transcribe any you think might be useful. Choose ads you think will suit your voice. Record and transcribe them on to your domestic machine to see how they sound, comparing your efforts with the working professionals. Don't worry about 'doing voices or accents' unless you are a brilliant mimic. Voice quality is largely what people are looking for, although genuine native accents are saleable too.

When you have found a few ads that suit you and worked on them, find a professional recording studio (these are advertised in *The Stage* or *Contacts*). Your efforts with amateur equipment at home will not be of a high enough quality. Ask to hear some of their tapes before committing yourself. I have heard some excellent ones made by Stephen Chase at Rhubarb Productions (9–15 Neal Street, Covent Garden, London WC2H 9PW Tel: 020 7836 1336). He runs workshops to help you prepare, manage and maintain your voice, identify its strengths and understand where it fits in the current marketplace. This is followed by a studio session to produce a professionally mastered broadcast-quality demo. (At the time of writing this package costs £250 + VAT.) Bernard Shaw, Horton Manor, Canterbury CT4 7LG Tel: 0122 7730843 e-mail: Bernardshaw-@talk21.com also provides a high-class and reasonably priced service, including six hours' studio time, free tea, sandwiches and Anadin! (£200 + VAT). You will find more information on his website – www.bernardshaw.co.uk. I would also highly recommend his book, *Voice-Overs – a Practical Guide* (published by A. & C. Black) – the first and only British book dealing exclusively and comprehensively with the skills, techniques and realities of the voice-over world. Both offer advice, provide scripts if you need them, and take time and care in directing the work. The studio will add appropriate jingles, sound effects and music to your work, making it as close as it could possibly be to a professional production.

When you have done your session the recording studio should supply you with your demo on a broadcast-quality CD or a master reel and several copies on cassette. The sound quality on CD is far better and most companies prefer to supply these. Stanley Productions (147 Wardour Street, London W1V 3TB Tel: 020 7439 0311) and East London Cassettes and Ideal Mastering (65–69 East Road, London N1 6AH Tel: 020 7251 6630) are two companies I know who will duplicate your CD for you (£160–£200 + VAT per hundred at the time of writing. The price generally includes 'on-body' printing and 'jewel cases'). They will also transfer your cassette on to CD.

If your demo *is* on tape you will be able to run off duplicates at home if you have the right equipment. If not, the recording studio will undertake cassette duplication for you, but at a price. If duplicating yourself, use C15 (ferric) tapes, which are cheap (at the time of writing around 40p each + VAT from Stanley Productions). These run for seven and a half minutes on each side, which will be sufficient for your purposes. You will need about a hundred copies to cover the ground, but it is probably better to run them off as and when you need them, so that if you get work you can update your demo without too much wastage.

Label the tape (not the cassette box) with your name, contact address and voice type (see pages 136–7). If you want your demo to look classy, inlay cards cost around 30p each for black and white, 50p each for colour. Or make them yourself. It's cheaper!

Showreels

If you want to work on screen, you need to be seen on screen, working. A professionally produced showreel is as important to an actor seeking screen work as professionally shot photographs.
Simon Hicks (Video Casting Directory)

Very few people who sit down to watch showreels are looking for versatility. They are looking for the very best actor they can get to play the bus conductress, the bank manager or a tramp. If they are casting a villain in a Bond movie, it's not helpful to see you presenting Blue Peter. *Some people who watch your showreel will luck imagination . . .*

Bill Thomas (actor, the plain vanilla video company)

A showreel is a video cassette, ideally no more than seven minutes long and no less than three, showing a number of clips from your work on camera. A showreel can have a number of purposes:

- packaging English stars for the American market where they may be largely unknown
- altering perceptions about an actor's work
- introducing new talent to the marketplace
- updating and reminding casting personnel of current work
- the ghastly business of trying to interest a new agent.

You may be lucky enough to have TV and film experience, in which case a video company can creatively edit together the best extracts of your work. A showreel can magnify the prospects of even very established performers.

NB: To get the best results when recording your work from TV, make sure you use top-quality videotape. If you don't get a good signal on your TV set, ask someone who does to record it for you.

You can use a mixture of edited and newly recorded material, but if you have no screen experience, you will need to track down a professional showreel company to make one for you from scratch. You will find half a dozen or so companies listed in the classified advertisements in *The Stage*. Ask around. Find out which one agents use for their clients. Equity, *Spotlight* and the Actors Centre will recommend the best. Others advertise with some of the casting information providers and in *Contacts*, etc. Video Casting Directory Ltd, 1 Triangle House, 2 Broomfield Road, London SW18 4HX Tel: 020 8874 3314 is one of the leaders in the field, with glowing recommendations from such luminaries as Miriam Margolyes, Bernard Holley, John Woodvine and Trevor Peacock. I have seen many of their showreels and would highly recommend their work. At the other end of the market I've seen excellent work by Bill Thomas (the plain vanilla company, 57 Purdy Street, London E1 3PD Tel: 020 7515 4865) and David Quilter (Quilter-Stott Productions, 22 Sherlock Court, Dorman Way, London NW8 ORU Tel: 07973 222 407) – both actors – who will edit your showreel for you from their homes. Both are relaxed and extremely reasonable. Both say 'if you don't like it you don't pay'. David Quilter will also help you shoot a short scene. He currently makes himself available for pre-production meetings at no charge. (The new digital technology makes this operation much more viable, flexible and cost-effective. Small cameras and computerised editing enable faster production and higher quality.)

Casting directors often ask to see showreels; most good agents expect their clients to provide one. Some actors have secured representation on the basis of them. Out-of-town theatres and casting personnel often use them as a cheap alternative to paying fares – or as a preview before deciding to audition or interview.

Although rarely a substitute for an audition, your showreel can be your ticket through the door, so make sure it is entertaining, dynamic, witty, varied, flowing and informative, with lots of good close-ups. It must look as if it has been edited from real on-screen performances, not your audition portfolio. It is a 'trailer' for your work. Casting directors will probably make a decision about your work in the first thirty seconds, so you need to engage their attention quickly. Put your best work at the beginning.

If you choose wisely, making your showreel is in itself an oppportunity to explore the medium and to get useful experience in front of a camera with a director. Reputable companies will offer a consultation session (for a fee) where your requirements will be discussed and ideas generated. This is well worth doing as a small outlay (around £30) may save you from making an expensive mistake. You should be clear and specific about your needs and listen carefully to any advice you might be given. You should take along any material you wish to prepare and any material you have on tape that you feel could be included.

The more work you have done in terms of identifying music, finding suitable props, costumes, locations, etc. and rehearsing your scenes, the more money you will save. Shooting and editing are generally charged by the hour, so it is important to plan your session carefully, although you may be able to negotiate a reduction for a whole day. You should leave questions of lighting and overdubbing (sound effects) to the studio. The consultation session will be an opportunity to ask some important questions:

- **Find out** what kind of tape your showreel will be shot on. Highband U-Matic SP (Special Performance) is the nearest to broadcast quality at the best price. Avoid companies offering VHS or Hi-8. VHS will not be good enough. The sound on Hi-8 will be hollow and echoey. You may be offered Betacam, which is even better quality than Highband but more expensive and may not be necessary for this purpose. Most digital formats are good – including mini DV.
- **Clarify** the degree of direction you are likely to get. The most reputable companies will be keen to show you examples of their work. Ideally, the director will be someone with strong experience on screen projects (ask to see his CV). Additional experience in the theatre would indicate an ability to support and enable your work. Request a meeting before the shoot and make sure the director sees your script before the session.
- **Ask** for a rundown on prices. Is VAT included? How much do additional copies cost? Companies that are prepared to be flexible about financing your showreel are generally on your side.
- **Choose** scenes for your showreel that suit you. The studio may have scripts and suggestions. They will advise you on whether the quality and format of the tapes or previous work are suitable for editing and inclusion. Once more, casting personnel will be looking for types, so play to your strengths. The object of the showreel is to show your talents as a screen actor. Choose extracts from TV scripts or screenplays that you might realistically be

asked to play. Chunks from stage plays rarely work on camera unless they are lit and shot as film.

Making a showreel can be expensive. The cost will vary wildly depending on its length and complexity. If you have little or no material on video you might expect to pay around £650 per day plus VAT for studio or location shooting. Editing and compilation is charged by the hour too (around £100 plus VAT). Captions or credits can be added for a modest extra cost and will make your showreel look very professional. It is generally the performer's responsibility to obtain and cover the cost of all necessary permissions and copyright clearances for any music or text that is used. Make sure you clear these well in advance. Copyright holders can be very tardy when only small sums of money are involved.

Extra VHS copies of your showreel can be purchased when you need them. Stanley Productions charges around £2.50 + VAT per copy for a five-minute showreel. They will also transfer your VHS copy on to CD-ROM (for which there is a growing demand, costing around £35 for the mastering, then circa £2.75 per copy + VAT. Transfer from VHS to NTSC (the American standard format for dispatch to Hollywood!) will cost approximately £7 + VAT per copy. These are prices for ten copies, but the more you copy the cheaper it becomes. Several companies do offer special discounts and student rates but this is not something to do 'on the cheap'. I cannot express strongly enough how important it is to do thorough research before committing yourself to such a major outlay.

The video demo-tape you did for me has made an AMAZING difference to my professional life ... after your compilation was seen in America, I was cast by Martin Scorsese, Lawrence Kasdan, Jonathan Wachs, Jay Leno, Ed Zuick and many TV people ...

(Extract from a letter to the Video Casting Directory from
Miriam Margolyes)

Keeping the cost to a minimum

- Scrutinise all your work on film, TV, corporate video, student film, etc. with a critical eye. Identify all the scenes that favour you, close-ups, reaction shots, etc. Keep an eye on your video counter and keep a note – so you can locate them later.
- Hire or borrow a complimentary video machine and connect it to your machine (video 1) with a scart lead, then using the RECORD and PAUSE button on the second machine (video 2), transfer all the chosen material on to a MASTER. It will be difficult to edit precisely to a frame, but you will now have all your best work on one tape.
- Scrutinise your MASTER. Can you make witty or dramatic connections between scenes? Are there good places to make edits? A head turn. A door slam. A walk out of shot. Look for drama, emotion, imaginative camera work, texture, moments for a montage, a good beginning or ending. (Annette Badland's show-reel cuts from her as 'prisoner's wife' saying 'another day up the judge's arse' to her as 'barrister' in a court-room drama with Joely Richardson.) The more familiar you become with your material, the more your creative juices will flow.
- Do you have a longish establishing close-up to run under your opening caption? Alternatively you can put your opening caption over a 10 x 8 photograph.
- Do you have material for an opening montage? This can be an intercut compilation of images taken from commercials, corporates, student films, dramas, etc. Perhaps six quick images quirkily cut together. It's all in the editing! You can use the images without the soundtrack and add your own sound later. A friend ran Beethoven's Ninth under her opening montage and very effective it was too!
- When you have made decisions about the most imaginative way to edit your material together, do a 'paper edit' – i.e. write down the order of the images and scenes you want to use, not forgetting to make a note of the video-counter numbers at the beginning and the end of each.

- Place your MASTER into video 1 and, using the RECORD and PAUSE button on video 2, rough-edit your material together in the order you want it. You will lose some quality along the way, but you will now begin to see what your showreel could look like.
- If you have an agent, ask his advice and make changes accordingly. It's his job to sell you. Make sure your showreel reinforces your marketing image.

With luck, you should now be in a position to take your 'rough edit', your 'paper edit' and your original tapes along to be edited in a professional editing suite (some advertise in *Contacts*). You will save a great deal of money if you know exactly what you want beforehand. It is a time-consuming process, but well worth the effort!

What if I don't have enough material?

If you don't have enough material for your showreel, you need to consider shooting additional footage to flesh it out. (I know actors who have created an entire showreel themselves and got work!)

Shooting your own footage
Scripts

Before you start, you need to find some suitable scripts. What are the genres in which you are most likely to get work? Cops and robbers, drama documentaries, sitcoms, soaps, modern drama, costume drama, action movies, war films, horror films, corporates, training films? Watch TV and film, and speculate on which parts you might be cast for. The likelihood of you playing Falstaff on screen is negligible. Be realistic!

You can (1) write your own script, (2) adapt from ideas on film or TV, (3) adapt from novels, (4) script from improvisations, or (5) commission a writer (an expensive option).

Scripts don't have to be long. Thirty seconds is enough to show what you can do. This short scene was written for a couple of my students – one a 'clean-cut copper' type, the other with a good line in young 'heavies'. Shoot it from both perspectives and each actor has a useful snippet for his showreel, giving a clear indication of his 'casting type'.

Ext. Doorway to a flat above a shop. Day

PC Copper *rings the doorbell quite hard. The door opens a chink. An unshaven young man in a 'boxer-style' dressing gown peers out.*

PC Copper   Mr Streetthug??

Streetthug *(the door opens wider, as do his eyes)*   Yeah ...

PC Copper   I wonder if I could have a word ...

Streetthug *(not shifting)*   Yeah?

PC Copper   We've had a complaint, sir ...

Streetthug   Nosy old bag upstairs, was it? Must be hearing things ...

PC Copper   ... we've had a complaint about shouting and banging about in your flat ... it's caused some alarm ... if I could just come in, I'm sure we can clear ...

Streetthug   I've told you ...

PC Copper *spots that* **Streetthug***'s knuckles are heavily grazed.*

PC Copper   Can I ask what happened to your hand, Mr Streethug?

Streetthug *(quickly withdrawing his hand, then aggressively)*   Look, I've just got up ... I don't need this ... there's no problem. No f***ing problem! OK?

He tries to slam the door. **PC Copper** *moves to stop him, but too late. The door is shut.*

A montage

If you are shooting images for your montage, they will look most effective if you set them in a context. Thus, talking to someone on your mobile in a shop doorway becomes an urgent call from your mother saying your father has been rushed to hospital. Play the situation and the moment will look real. If you are walking into shot, where are you coming from? If you are walking out of shot, where are you going to?

Locations

When deciding on scripts, make sure that scenes won't be too difficult to shoot. Keep locations simple. If you have set your heart on a ski-slope, you can always be shot against a blue screen and add the Himalayas later – the wizardry of digital computer technology – but it will be difficult to capture the atmosphere of icy wind and swirling snow! Choose locations to which you have free and legal access. Scenes in doorways, cars, markets, gardens, parks, Uncle Herbert's hardware shop, a friend's posh kitchen. Single-handed scenes on the telephone/mobile are ideal. They can be imbued with drama and shot in close-up, indoors or out. If you are shooting several scenes, make sure locations are close together. It's time-consuming and expensive to trek equipment and crew from Hampstead Heath to Balham. Use your imagination. Your home has many rooms, a front door, a garden, a rose arch, a brick wall, a bench, windows to look in through/out of, corridors, broom cupboards, the road outside, a garage, tables outside your local pub, a friendly local shop, etc. etc. With a bit of imaginative dressing, a corner can become an office, a fake gasfire and hairy rug the scene of flickering seduction!

Costumes, wigs and make-up

You can hire full outfits, individual items like handbags and feather boas, wigs, props, etc. by the week and at modest cost (see *Contacts* for a long list of companies that specialise). I have found Cosprop (Tel: 020 7485 6731) and Angels and Bermans (Tel: 020 7387 0999) – both in London – extremely accommodating, with extensive choice. Don't hire a whole costume if you are only shooting from the waist up! If your scene is not set in the present, *research your period*. Pay attention to detail. Modern make-up and a 1960s frock will spoil the effect. Make sure each scene is costumed and propped to perfection. Would your character read those books in the bookcase behind you? Is that the kind of briefcase a solicitor would carry?

Once you have your scripts and have located everything you need, REHEARSE, REHEARSE and REHEARSE. Rehearse until your little scripts are in your bones and nothing will distract you short of Armageddon. *It is the quality of your work on screen that will get you that job. Make it the very best you can do.*

Choose actors to work with who are as good as you. If you have a willing high-profile friend, so much the better. The better the actors you work with, the better you will be.

You need to get your ball back!

Make sure other actors are as right for their parts as you are for yours.

Compile a detailed shooting schedule, keeping in mind the simplicity of costume changes, the quality of the light and the ease of movement between locations. Arrange for there to be somewhere on location to hang costumes, a dressing table and well-lit mirror to apply make-up, and a long mirror to see the full effect. Make sure you leave sufficient time between scenes in your schedule to move location, set up, change costume, hair and make-up, and centre yourself for your performance.

Now you are ready to shoot! Here are a few websites you might find useful:

www.ukscreen.com
http://www.shootingpeople.org/
http://www.mandy.com/
http://www.geocities.com/SoHo/Studios/8451/

Click on to these and you should be able to make links with other useful sites, and access equipment and skilled freelancers with time and commitment to spare. Many young film-makers (directors, camera-men, sound engineers, editors, etc.) are seeking opportunities to showcase their own work, so you will be able to help each other out!

I found the whole experience of producing and editing my own showreel both satisfying and enthralling. I'd recommend it to anyone. By thinking and planning laterally, my three-and-a-half-minute showreel came in at below £400. I've already had positive feedback from several major casting directors, the BBC and elsewhere – honestly, much more effective than just sending out a CV and photograph!

Claude Starling (actor)

3 Advertising your Product

You have a product to sell. How does a potential customer know what it looks like or where to find it? It pays to advertise, and there is one essential publication in which your details should feature: *Spotlight*.

Spotlight

Spotlight
7 Leicester Place
London WC2H 7BP
Tel: 020 7437 7631
Fax: 020 7437 5881
e-mail: info@spotlightcd.com
website: www.spotlightcd.com

The most important casting directory in the United Kingdom and probably the most successful in the world is *Spotlight*. It would be fair to describe it as a benign monopoly in as much as it seems to have 'seen off' all serious competitors by virtue of its longevity, comprehensiveness and accuracy.

If you are serious about your career, you certainly need to have an entry in *Spotlight*.

Spotlight describes the publication as 'part of the bloodstream of the profession'. It was founded in 1927 by a stage manager called Keith Moss in the days when there was no TV and few actors' agents. Managements would lay out actors' photographs on the floor and walk between the rows to choose a cast! To avoid this cumbersome procedure Keith Moss thought of publishing a directory in which working actors of the day were persuaded to advertise. Sybil Thorndike as St Joan appeared in the first slim edition.

What began as a book of photographs became a massive database of additional information about agents, credits and skills. Today there are four volumes of *Spotlight Actors*, four volumes of *Spotlight Actresses*, a CD-ROM published quarterly and a live, continuously updated internet service, *Spotlight Casting Live*. *Spotlight* has an unparalleled distribution network throughout the world and the books, CD and Internet access are purchased by legitimate casting directors, advertising agencies, film producers, managements – indeed, anyone with a professional interest in casting. If you want exposure to people making decisions, you need to be in *Spotlight*; it is on every computer terminal at the BBC, for example.

Actors can be searched by past performances – credits, productions, directors – by performance skills, musical or dance skills, physical attributes such as hair colour or height and many more criteria too lengthy to mention here. To appear in *Spotlight* you need to complete two forms: a book entry form and a digital (CD/Internet) entry form on which you can record this search criteria and up to twenty credits. Your book entry consists of your stage name, a good, sharply focused headshot and your agent's contact details. Directories are divided into categories – leading character, younger character and young – so you can be published in the section most appropriate to your casting profile.

As an actor appearing in *Spotlight* you are provided with two security numbers with which to access your details on the Internet. Using your security numbers you (or your agent) can update credits or skills at any time from anywhere in the world with computer access as often as you like. *Spotlight Casting Live*: this award-winning Internet version of the famous *Spotlight* casting directories is very live; it can be accessed twenty-four hours a day and updated continuously twenty-four hours a day. Technological advances mean your face can be seen in New York and your voice can be heard in Los Angeles or Perth. *Spotlight* can include up to four thirty-second voice clips and are ready to include movement as soon as they feel the quality of Internet broadcasts is acceptable. At the time of writing it is *Spotlight*'s view that Internet broadcasts are unreliable, so they are not encouraging actors to spend money producing videotapes which are rarely, if ever, viewed and when broadcasts across the Internet do not enhance the actor.

In 2001 the *Spotlight Link* was launched, which is a free Internet breakdown service for casting directors and agents. A casting director is able to send a breakdown via e-mail to agents who can respond with suggestions of actors to be cast in the prescribed roles. When an agent receives a breakdown, their list of clients in *Spotlight* automatically appears on screen with photographs and all they need to do is select those actors they feel might be suitable. (So if you're not in *Spotlight* you won't appear.) Feature films, stage plays and commercials are all travelling across the *Spotlight Link* and thousands of actors have already been proposed in this way. If you are currently without an agent, fear not. Another new development is the provision of free casting information to actors in *Spotlight*: *Spotlight* encourages the casting industry to post forthcoming opportunities (which you would normally only be able to access in subscriber-only publications) on *Spotlight Bulletin* so actors can view it free of charge.

Spotlight actors are included in Artists' Records, a telephone enquiry service that answers thousands of calls a day and is now freely available at www.spotlightcd.com. This service instantly locates the agent of every artist in *Spotlight*.

All this promotion costs £95 per year plus VAT. I have always found personnel at *Spotlight* to be extremely helpful and supportive, and they provide a free telephone service to actors in *Spotlight*.

Spotlight also publishes *Spotlight Graduates*, a directory of graduates from accredited drama schools forming the Conference of Drama Schools, *Spotlight Presenters*, *Spotlight Children and Young Performers*, *Walk-on and Supporting Artists* and *Spotlight Index*, a complete list of actors and actresses in *Spotlight*.

Women need to deliver their entries to *Spotlight* by 1 May, men by 1 November and children by 15 November, and the relevant *Spotlight* is published in six months – but your entry can be included on the

Internet at any time of year and will automatically go into the next book.

Ugly Agency

The Ugly Agency Ltd
Tigris House
256 Edgware Road
London W2 1DS
Tel: 020 7402 5564
Fax: 020 7402 0507
e-mail: info@ugly.org
website: www.ugly.org

The Ugly Agency was started in 1969 by a photographer and two advertising executives who were frustrated by the shortage of everyday, man/woman-in-the-street faces available for their work through the model agencies. Their models are not necessarily 'ugly' (whatever that means) but simply have character or embody a certain type. Flick through the directory and you will find everything from celebrity lookalikes, 'wee folks', boffins and stilt-walking uni-cyclists to twins and 'the girl next door' types. All human life is there. The *Ugly Casting Directory* is dispatched free and on request to anyone looking for faces. Although it is essentially a model agency, quite a number of actors appear in it and find small parts in TV and film, rock videos and advertisements. 'Someone from Ugly is in nearly every commercial you see,' claims the agency's managing director.

Actors pay a fee for the inclusion of three photographs in the *Directory*, which is updated every two years.

Back in the late 1960s I was a great admirers of Pasolini's films, so in 1970, I think it was, as a rookie actor I was very excited when he came to Britain to make his version of Canterbury Tales. *I was certain I was natural material for him and furthermore I belonged to a model/*

actor's agency called 'Ugly' that specialised in ordinary people, eccentrics and 'character faces', and was the first port of call for film-makers looking for such things. Sure enough, Pasolini swanned in, picked a dozen or so people from the agency's books and swanned out again. Surely I was one of the elect? I was not! Determined to correct this outrageous mistake, I duly turned up uninvited at the casting session.

The casting director was a formidable mid-Atlantic matron, well-known and feared in the business, and she was there in person. Taking advantage of a gap in the proceedings, I presented myself at the door of the interview room and announced my name. Strangely, it wasn't down on her list. 'Really? But it should be there.' (Of course it should.) And such was my conviction that she hesitated and rechecked. In the meantime I could see in the background Pasolini's impish head as he craned this way and that trying to get a better look at me. Just as the great lady's lips were setting firm again, the great man spoke. 'Scusi, scusi, vieni, vieni, per favore,' or whatever it is they say in Italy and he waved me in.

I sat opposite him over a desk. He grinned mischievously at me and said gleefully to an assistant, 'Poor lecher.' No, he wasn't being personal, that was the part I was being offered. Delighted, I agreed at once, whereupon several acolytes swarmed all over me with tape measures and Polaroid cameras.

As I left, I didn't even notice the casting lady I was so elated. Was she peeved? I don't know. The whole 'audition' had taken, perhaps, three minutes.

David Hatton (actor)

4 Selling your Product

You have developed your 'brand image', assembled a professional 'marketing package' and advertised your 'product'. The time has come to try your product in the marketplace.

The problem for most actors is not 'playing the part' but getting the opportunity in the first place. 'How do I get an audition?' is the general cry. 'I know I could get the job if only I could be seen!' Many actors feel an agent is the best salesman for their wares.

Wherever two or more actors are gathered together, knotty questions about agents will always arise. How can I persuade an agent to take me on? How will I know if they are working for me? Why do they never ring? Are casting directors prejudiced against co-operative agencies? How will I know which agent is any good? Finding a halfway decent agent is an actor's nightmare.

Agencies

Changing agents is like changing deckchairs on the Titanic!

Noel Coward

Top-flight agencies only represent actors with established reputations and the brightest and most talented newcomers from the leading drama schools. They can take their pick of the profession and there is little point in courting them unless you have already achieved some success. A broad range of agencies varying dramatically in size and reputation represent the body of working actors in the profession and include co-operative agencies (see page 51) which have been in existence since the 1970s.

The most highly regarded agents have modest, but carefully selected, client registers, representing no more than a couple of dozen actors. Each client will be hand-picked and carefully targeted at a specific area of work. For instance, they might represent one young leading man, one glamorous grandmother, one freckled teenage boy and so on. There will be no clashes and very little overlap in the kind of client they represent.

There are also specialist agencies dealing solely with voice-overs or commercial casting. Others represent specific groups like presenters, DJs, dancers, choreographers, models, after-dinner speakers, extras, ethnic minorities, etc.

The larger agencies can sometimes represent several hundred clients. They have an unselective client list and will rarely ask to see your work before offering to represent you. They make their commission by submitting several clients for the same job in the hope that one of them will strike lucky. Something of a cattle market! They often ask for a joining fee or fee for inclusion in their agency directory.

Patently, some agencies are much more highly regarded than others, although this hierarchy is continually shifting, depending on the quality of performer the agency has been able to attract. Reputations, both good and bad, often linger despite changes in circumstances so it is always wise to talk to other actors about their experiences before making any decision about representation.

What makes a good agent?

A good agent can fulfil some very useful functions and offer invaluable advice and support. He should have an abundance of business sense and advise you on your CV, your photograph, your demo-tape and your showreel. He should be objective, professional and nurturing, and always find time to talk to you about your career. (If he is discourteous or offhand with you he may be less than appealing to casting personnel.) He should be honest and constructive about your work.

He must have personal contacts in all areas, be a dedicated

theatregoer and keep abreast of the contemporary scene, regularly mailing casting personnel to keep them informed of clients' activities. He should press casting personnel to come and see your work, and always be there to support you and entertain them, no matter how many times he has to sit through an uncut *Man and Superman*.

Ideally, he will have a small stable of working actors on his books, none of whom clash too seriously with you. When he submits you for a job he should be courteous enough to inform you if he is submitting another of his clients for the same part.

The submissions he makes on your behalf should be accurate and targeted, so that you can have the best possible chance of success. You have a right to know the jobs you are being submitted for, so that you can make a reasonable assessment of the work he is doing on your behalf. An agent who is cagey or secretive about submissions probably isn't making many.

> *One of the Ten Commandments of the good agent is Thou Shalt, under all circumstances, try to see thy people work unless there is a very good reason not to. I do think you owe them that, whether they are on the fringe or in something more prestigious – and if at all possible, take a casting director, kicking and screaming, with you . . .*
> Suzanne Alvarez (Alvarez Management)

If your agent refuses to take commission on work you find yourself and has a compassionate view on taking commission for overtime he is a rare, scrupulous and wonderful creature.

On the other hand, if he takes you on without seeing your work and asks for money for the privilege, he is clearly more interested in the cash than in the client. (A co-op will legitimately ask for money.)

Be very wary of an agent who has so many people on his books that it would take a small battalion to represent them. If he hedges his bets, submits several clients for the same part and makes inaccurate and inept submissions to casting personnel, he probably has neither the time nor the resources to aid your career in the manner you would wish. You are better off handling your own affairs!

The perception that once an actor has an agent he can sit back and wait for the phone to ring is very far from the truth. Like a marriage, you will both have to work hard to make the relationship mutually beneficial.

> *Actors feel very insecure when other actors say, 'Hasn't your agent put you up for that? Everybody has been seen for it!' Or 'How much are you getting? My agent got a very good deal!' Actors listen to other actors rather than discussing concerns with their agents. Obviously it's in their agents' best interest to help them get work and negotiate the best fees. You're supposed to be on the same side!*
> Jennifer Jaffrey (Magnolia Management)

How to find an agent

You will find a comprehensive list of agents in *Contacts* and *Spotlight* will supply you with a list of reputable agents with current gaps in their client registers. There are frequent advertisements in *The Stage*, the *Equity Journal* or on the Actors Centre Notice Board. Smaller agencies and co-ops often have gaps for ethnic minorities or actors over fifty. Genuine Geordies seem to be at a premium across the board.

Once you have identified some agents that interest you (and whom you feel you might interest), submit your marketing package. Your letter should be short and informative, setting out why you are seeking representation and what you have to offer. You may be one of a dozen actors whose particulars drop through the letter box on any given day, so it is important that yours attracts attention. Enclose your showreel, your demo-tape, reviews of your stage work or a copy of a well-made student film. Needless to say, the best time to approach an agent is when you are working.

One agent I know was impressed by an actor who boldly announced he was 'seeking representation' in the programme of a fringe show. She liked his work. She liked his style. She took him on!

Agents are impressed by actors who are proactive about their careers, so make it clear from the start that you are prepared to make the necessary investment of both time and money.

If an agent is impressed with your application, you may be invited into the office for an initial interview, but most good agents will, quite rightly, want to see you work before offering to represent you. Inform those agents who have responded positively to your original package as soon as you land a decent part on stage, on TV, or in film. Send a further copy of your CV and photograph along with any promotional material, fliers, etc. you have about the job to reinforce the impression you have made.

Alternatively, some agents hold 'audition days' if they have a gap in their client list, to assess the skills of actors that interest them. This is one way of seeing actors work. Auditions can be quite sophisticated, involving improvisation, a singing audition and work with a director. Actors who impress can be offered representation.

Other agents have been known to take clients on the basis of a strong recommendation from a respected employer. Sometimes an excellent showreel can work the miracle.

How to get the best out of your agent

- Provide a high-quality CV, a selection of photographs, a demo-tape, a showreel and a contact list of directors who already know your work, so that your agent can present the highest professional profile on your behalf.
- Be brief and to the point when you call the office. Don't hassle!

It's depressing to be told each week that you have been submitted for fifteen-to-twenty roles but that casting directors have not thought you suitable for a single audition! Most good agents diligently keep lists of all productions clients have been submitted for. I certainly do. But it would be time-consuming and counter-productive to report back to clients all the time. If they haven't had an audition for several months – then a polite call would be a good idea. Actors should learn to trust their agents. If they don't, they shouldn't have asked them to represent them in the first place.

Jennifer Jaffrey (Magnolia Management)

- Be prepared with polished audition pieces for all occasions.

- Hone your sight-reading techniques.
- Be available. Actors must work in other areas to pay the bills, but if you turn down that small-scale theatre tour in favour of a lucrative temping job, your agent will soon stop taking you seriously.
- Don't talk money. That's your agent's job.

> *Years ago I was up for the lead part in* Poldark, *a major new drama series about to be made by the BBC. I was chatting away to the producer who asked me if I'd done much for the BBC. 'Yes,' I said, 'I've done a couple of things and I've always worked for the Chinese accountant Special Low. And I hope in my next job I'll be working for his brother Special High.' Robin Ellis got the part* . . .
>
> Gareth Hunt (actor)

- Take careful notes about jobs and addresses. Your agent has better things to do than respond to frantic last-minute calls from your mobile asking where you were supposed to be at two o'clock.
- Be punctual for auditions and interviews you are sent for. Don't ask your agent to change appointments if you can possibly help it. Be seen to be keen. If you don't want the job, don't go to the audition. Refusing a job when offered reflects badly on the agency.
- Be clean, smart, polite and courteous at all times. Your behaviour reflects on the agency and can either enhance or damage the chances of other clients. A reputation for 'being difficult' spreads quickly. Most directors would rather hire a lesser talent who is an unselfish joy to work with than a fiery genius who upsets other actors, wastes time and turns rehearsals into a breathing nightmare.
- Give ample warning about the date of your First Night. You can't expect busy people to drop everything at a moment's notice.
- Keep the office informed of your whereabouts so you can be contacted at a moment's notice.
- Be loyal. It seems that as soon as actors achieve success they feel 'it's time to move on'. Agents hate that phrase. Actually, it's probably the time to *stay*! Especially when an agent knows you, has nurtured you and helped develop your career. The 'time to

move on' is when the relationship is not working for either of you.
• Value your agent's judgement and any advice he has to offer.

What about a co-operative agency?

A job for one is a victory for us all!
Penny Macdonald (Heavy Pencil Management Co-operative)

A co-operative agency (co-op) is essentially a group of actors working as agents for themselves. Clients of a co-op are known as 'members'. Members represent each other in the marketplace, finding work and negotiating deals for other members. A co-operative agency takes a percentage of the fee for each job acquired for its members in the same way a conventional agency does. Co-operatives operate on the principle of one member, one vote. Employers are also employees and vice versa, and all profits are redistributed for the common good. Successful co-ops can invest surplus funds in office refurbishment, upgraded technology or pay for everybody's *Spotlight* advertisement.

Many actors prefer co-ops to a conventional agency. It gives them a unique opportunity to work in supportive groups and have a hands-on influence over their own careers.

Most co-ops have around twenty members. A larger group is unwieldly and difficult to service, and if membership is too small and most members are working it may be difficult to service the office.

Members may range between those committed to the idea and ideal of creating the best possible agent for themselves and those who see the co-op as a stepping stone to what they consider 'a real agent'. The latter are not generally popular with other co-op members!

Co-operative agencies began to emerge in the 1970s and were rooted in the caring and sharing principles of the wider co-operative movement. They attracted a largely young, energetic, idealistic and committed membership. ICOM (the Industrial Common Ownership Movement at 74 Kirkgate, Leeds LS2 7DJ Tel: 0113 246 1737 Fax: 0113 244 0002) is a membership organisation with the primary aim of promoting democratic control of enterprises by the people who work in them and the principles and practice of common ownership. If you want to set up your own co-op they will advise you on how to proceed and help you choose between the various legal structures that are available.

The first co-operative agency for actors, Actorum (Actors' Forum), began with a few actors sitting round a table with a telephone. It now occupies offices just off Oxford Street, serviced by state-of-the-art technology and representing around two dozen members!

Membership of a co-op is particularly useful to actors 'starting out', although many older actors prefer this way of working too. No more waiting for the telephone to ring! No more worries about what submissions an oddly silent agent is making on your behalf! Members have instant access to all the information from the casting information providers such as *SBS* (see page 69) as well as the support and advice of their colleagues. Furthermore, the commitment that every member has to make towards the smooth running of the office can dispel some of the isolation that every actor is familiar with.

These days co-operatives are as selective about their client lists as conventional agents are. Some very successful actors have been represented by them (Julie Walters and Pete Postlethwaite come to mind). Each co-op will have developed its own criteria for accepting or rejecting members. If they are interested, most co-ops will interview you, but like conventional agents they will generally defer a decision as to whether or not to take you on until after they have seen you work. You may also be asked to work in the office for a day or two to see how you fit in before they make a final decision.

Secretarial and negotiating skills are almost as important to a co-op as acting talent. Business ability is increasingly sought by co-ops wishing to maximise their effectiveness within limited resources. If you become a member, you will be jointly responsible for every aspect of the smooth running of the agency, from ensuring the telephone bills are paid and the office equipment is regularly serviced to calculating commission and interviewing prospective members.

Although there is less prejudice than there used to be among casting personnel towards co-ops, some still acknowledge a twinge of embarrassment at finding themselves in head-to-head negotiation with an actor whose work they may not like or whom they may have rejected for another job. But in a buyer's market co-ops are just as aware of the importance of good presentation, strong marketing skills and efficient management as traditional agencies.

If you are invited to join a co-op you may be asked for a modest joining fee. This will be your contribution towards the cost of printing their particulars and to the running costs of the agency. It may be anything between £150 and £300. Some co-ops treat fifty per cent of this sum as a 'returnable deposit', which you can reclaim if and when you leave. The more financially successful co-ops don't need to do this. Others will take on a batch of new clients if they are a bit short of money, so that's certainly something to be wary of.

The most common problem expressed by co-ops is the difficulty in holding members' meetings when many of the co-op's members are working at different times, often miles from where it is based.

Negotiating your contract with an agent

When any agent takes you on, make sure you are supplied with a contract setting out clearly the nature of your relationship, the commission that will be charged for theatre, TV, commercials, etc., how it will be collected and the terms of termination for both parties. Generally agents will charge a flat rate of ten per cent commission on stage, radio and video work, and twelve and a half per cent on television, commercials and films. Some agents might charge a higher rate of fifteen per cent on West End work and large-scale tours. Beware of any agent who wants any more than this!

Regulation of agencies

There are a number of ways of ensuring that an agency is reputable. *Spotlight* will advise you. Membership of the Personal Managers' Association (PMA 0208 398 9796) offers some guidance, although not all good agents are members. The PMA has a code of conduct with regard to the way members operate and will investigate if they receive complaints. Equity does not recommend agents, but at the back of the *Equity Journal* is a 'Special Attention' list of people against most of whom Equity has outstanding actions. Equity has also published a code of conduct very similar to that of the PMA, which provides a standard agreement for actors to sign with their agents together with a leaflet advising you on the nature of your contractual relationship with them.

Since the enactment of the Deregulation and Contracting Out Act 1994, actors' agents (along with all employment agencies) can now legally operate without licence. The effect of this has been the mushrooming of small agencies. Anyone can now set up as an actor's agent, regardless of their background. Before the Act was passed the Department of Employment could withdraw the licences of exploitative or crooked agencies. While there was clearly never any defence against unscrupulous agents defecting to South America with the contents of their client account, those accounts *were* kept separate by law under the terms of the old Employment Act, giving clients some small protection.

Can I get work without an agent?

Yes, you can, but you will need to be very hardworking, creative and determined. An agent has a developed network of contacts and inside information about forthcoming productions, which you are not likely to be able to match. Without an agent, you need to build your own contact list and database from scratch.

Even if you do have an agent it will be beneficial to supplement his activities in as many ways as you can. However active he might be on your behalf, nobody can have a greater interest in your career than you. You are the interface between your purchaser and your product, and the most dynamic thing you can do for your flagging self-esteem is to put your back into selling it.

There is nothing more enervating than waiting for the phone to ring; nothing is more energising than feeling you have taken your destiny into your own hands!

Making contacts

Contacts are one of an actor's most vital resources. They are gold dust. But where do you begin?

Friends and colleagues in the business are an invaluable source of information. Make it your business to follow up any lead, however small. 'Did you know so-and-so was casting such-and-such ... ?' 'Wotsit's film has been deferred until next June.' Don't be afraid to make a telephone call to find out more. If you have an agent, ensure he is aware of every contact you make, so that he can follow them up and capitalise on them as well. Make a note of every contact he makes too.

> *I watch television programmes to see where the best opportunities might be for a disabled person and make notes – then, together with my agent, we target those. I have to target the work. It would be stupid just to go for everything. I also sit on a number of committees like the One in Eight Group, which is attended by Charles Denton, former Head of Drama at the BBC, independent producers, writers, actors, directors, and network through them like mad ... I have also set up my own production company, so I meet people in connection with that. I cannot rely totally on being a performer. Every performer out there knows how hard it is and it is doubly hard when you are in a wheelchair. I am not going to sit back and wait for the phone call. I have to make things happen. And if that means concentrating on other things I can do as well as acting – like presenting – then that's what I'm going to do.*
>
> Julie Fernandez (actor)

Maintain contact with drama-school tutors who are active in the profession. Many are directors who also teach. Keep them informed about your work and keep an eye on theirs. They will know what you are capable of, which gives you a head start when they are casting.

When you are in a show, keep track of anyone useful who comes along to see it. Directors, casting directors, producers and agents often get complimentary tickets, so check with the box office to see who's been in. Share information with other performers and follow up every lead quickly before the memory fades. If you are generous to other actors, they will be generous to you.

Treat every audition as an opportunity to make a contact. Be methodical and professional. Keep a note of the director's name and write a brief note about the audition for your filing system as soon as you get home. What kind of work does he do? Follow up the audtion up with a short letter saying how much you enjoyed the meeting. If you don't get that job, write again in three months' time, remind him of your existence and ask if he is casting anything in the future you might be right for. (This is why you need a good paper or cyber filing/indexing system!) Pop in a fresh CV and photograph. Do this every time you audition and your contact list will grow.

Don't be afraid to name-drop. 'My friend Hermione Jobbing-Theatrical, who worked with you on *Up and at 'em* in January, tells me that you are casting a new sitcom set in an abattoir ... My father is a butcher ...' Every little helps and it makes you sound as if you are 'in the know'.

Make a list of all those directors you have worked with in the past. What are they doing now? When did you last write to them? If you haven't been in touch for some time, you may be surprised how pleased they are to hear from you, especially if you did good work together. Try 'I'll be passing TV Centre next Tuesday. I'd love to pop into your office to say hello ...' or 'I came across a still of me as Pope Joan the other day. Wasn't it fun? Are you ever free for a coffee?' Keep your eyes peeled for their work. If you like it, grab the opening to scribble a congratulatory little card.

Keep a record of anyone you meet at parties, workshops, first nights, the BBC Club, the Granada canteen, the Actors Centre Green Room, Joe Allen's, in the bar after a fringe show, etc. Today's fringe director is tomorrow's Artistic Director of the Royal Court Theatre! Theatre audiences are peopled by folk in the business, so make sure you are seen around. You'll be surprised how quickly people will start saying, 'Don't I know your face ... ?' Casting directors usually attend first and second nights. Make sure everyone you meet is the proud possessor of your business card.

It's as good as a postcard – a wave across the room!

Jan Younger (*Spotlight*)

Equity branch meetings, held monthly, are an excellent place to make contacts too. Equity will be happy to tell you when and where your local branch meets or you will find branches listed in your *Equity Journal* with information about meetings and future events. Meetings often attract a starry selection of guest speakers (my own local branch recently hosted the casting director of the National Theatre and representatives from a top commercial casting agency) and provide an opportunity to glean inside information from the horse's mouth and to make useful contacts as well. Casting personnel will be much more amenable if they've met and liked you than if you are just another unsolicited CV.

My aim, as Chair of the North-West London Branch of Equity, has always been that it should be a place for ideas, criticisms and making changes as well as socialising. The meetings are great for making contacts – we have guest speakers ranging from theatre and television directors to tax and insurance experts. Recently we have welcomed John Cannon, Head of Casting at the RSC, the playwright Olwen Wymark, Kate Rowland, Head of BBC Radio Drama, Lawrence Till, Artistic Director of the Palace Theatre, Watford, Nicholas Kent, Artistic Director of the Tricycle Theatre. Any Equity member will be welcomed at their local branch.

Diana Brookes (actor)

Don't be afraid to make contact by telephone, but do make sure you are feeling charming and confident before your pick up the receiver. One of my students, sceptical about my advice, took it upon himself to telephone a long list of casting directors I had given him. Far from receiving the cold shoulder he'd expected, he had a very encouraging reaction: many responded with either information about current work, a request for a CV and photograph or the suggestion that he should ring back in a few weeks' time.

If you want to get through to someone important, you mustn't be apologetic in your manner. You must speak with absolute confidence and conviction. Whenever I ring up I just say, 'It's Harry.' Eight times out of ten the secretary will put you through because they think that the person you are trying to get through to must know who you are and they don't dare ask.

Hariet Lake (actor)

Contacts

Spotlight also publishes another directory called *Contacts* (each new edition is published in October). It contains a comprehensive list of names, addresses and telephone numbers of theatre, television, film and radio companies, agents, drama schools, photographers, production companies, festivals, press cuttings, actors' agencies and personal managers, professional organisations – you name it. It is an invaluable reference book for all those in the acting profession.

Self-help Groups

A constructive by-product of my workshops at the Actors Centre has been the setting of up of a number of self-help groups where actors meet on a regular basis after the course. Each group organises itself in a way that suits it best. Some work co-operatively and share the responsibility for administration and small budgets. Some settle on more formal committee procedures with a chair, secretary and treasurer. Others see it is an opportunity for a good night out, a pint and a chat. Whatever the format, members report finding a new sense of belonging and focus.

An American actor told me about the support groups she had come across in Hollywood. There, each member must come armed with a piece of casting information to gain access. Not a bad idea!

The most effective groups tend to be the most organised ones. They fund the cost of running the group and the casting information sheets from a shared bank account or kitty, operating rather like an ad hoc co-operative agency. Details and guidance about casting information providers can be found on pages 185–6. The cost of photographers, studios, etc. is shared. Some collaborate on show-reels. Members are on the constant lookout for work for each other. Actors who are working bring in information gleaned from the rehearsal room or the studio floor. One member is deputed to ring round casting directors once a week and pool the information; another is dispatched to cull useful casting information from the Actors Centre Notice Board, the desk at *Spotlight* or *The Stage* and ring round the Castcall numbers (see page 72) or the Equity Job Information Line (see page 69). Groups put themselves on the mailing list of regional theatres. These give information about forthcoming productions so that actors can target submissions. Play texts are shared. Members make themselves available to hear audition pieces and advise on voice tapes and showreels.

One self-help group did so well it installed a fax and photocopier in a member's home and now operates as a fully-fledged actors' agency. Another shared the cost of mounting its own fringe production, which gave members a batch of excellent reviews, confidence, experience and another credit on the CV.

Casting Directors

I wrote an article on casting directors for Queen *or* Vogue, *I can't remember which. I was fascinated to know why so many casting directors are women and approached a doyenne of the profession – a very splendid lady. I asked her if it had ever happened that actors offered certain 'favours' for parts . . . She glared at me rather severely and said, 'You should not assume that if someone wants to go to bed with me it is merely because they want a part.' I left feeling very chastened.*

. . . I asked another the same question. 'Do you ever get offered bribes?' It seemed a perfectly proper question to ask. She sounded very cross. 'Of course not,' she said. 'I think I can honestly say that in all these years I've never been offered a bribe.' We were in the canteen of a big London theatre. At that very moment a young actor walking

*past our table dumped a tin of frankfurters in front of her and said,
'There you are, darling, I know you love these. I picked them up in
Germany . . .'*

David Benedictus (actor and novelist)

Casting directors are employed by directors and producers to find
the right actor for the right job in anything from a pop video to a
Merchant Ivory film. They are not actors' agents. A good casting
director is a file junkie with a computer for a brain and the memory
of an elephant. A high percentage of casting directors are women.

Casting directors make frequent visits to the theatre, watch
television and films, and attend end-of-year productions at the
leading drama schools. They are on a tireless quest for new faces and
exciting talent. Actors are their stock-in-trade: they collect them. At
best, a casting director has imagination, insight, the ability to think
laterally, interpersonal skills of a very high order and the hide of a
rhino.

A few of the larger theatres have their own casting directors.
Smaller theatres generally can't afford them. Increasingly now,
casting directors are freelances, on short-term contracts, brought in to
cast specific TV shows, commercials, films, etc. Gone are the days of
long-term contracts with TV companies – days of operating from
plush offices, all expenses paid. The recession, the 'contact culture'
and the legislative measures introduced in the mid-1980s have put
paid to that. Membership of ACTT (Association of Cinematographic
Television and Allied Technicians/BECTU Broadcasting Entertainment Cinematograph and Theatre Union) is no longer required.
There are more of them around, so work can be thin on the ground.

Casting directors can't get you a job – the director or producers
will have the final say on casting – but they can effect an introduction
and recommend your skills. After that, it's up to you. At the end of
the day, it's in their interest for you to be cast, for their submissions
to be successful, because that reflects favourably on their own skill
and perspicacity. They are just as likely to be unemployed after this
job as you are. A good casting director is a good actor's friend.

How can I be seen by a casting director?

Sometimes I get fifty or sixty requests a week to go and see things. There's only me. I can't see everything. But you know how much it means to actors to go – and you know how much it means to them if you stay behind and say hello. You can only do six a week, if that. It's very hard.

Kay Magson (Casting Director, West Yorkshire Playhouse)

Casting directors can't recommend you if they haven't seen you work – but how can you be seen if no one will cast you? Most actors could paper the loo wall with letters from casting directors that read:

> Dear Chrys Salt,
> Thank you so much for sending me your CV and photograph. Let me know when you are working and I will do my best to come and see you . .

'Chicken and egg!' I hear you cry.

Every casting director is inundated with enquiries. They are endlessly petitioned, coerced, courted and cajoled. (Don't send gifts. It places them in an invidious position.) Many can scarcely afford a secretary to cope with the avalanche of mail. Nevertheless, it is your job to ensure your CV and photo reach their desks and receive the consideration they deserve. Make sure you let casting directors know whenever you are appearing in something worthy of their attention. Their diaries fill up fast, so give them plenty of warning and you may be lucky. If your photograph is striking and your CV confirms your ability, quite a few casting directors will call you for interview.

I was asked to attend auditions for my musical Oscar. I'd never attended auditions before and thought it would be really great to be in on the casting side as well. When I arrived, the casting director gave me a typed sheet with everybody's name and audition time on it – all terribly professional with a space for comments – so I got my pen and sat there waiting to write loads and loads of comments in the comments section, not really knowing what sort of comments I should *write. Marks out of ten? Good, bad or indifferent? After writing a few nonsensical things I took a sneaky look at the person next to me for enlightenment and saw she'd written NFT, NFT, NFT ... I thought, That's so rude ... I just hope the actors don't walk over here and see that. I assumed it stood for 'No f***ing talent!' So embarrassing! Afterwards I said, 'Don't you try to keep these comments away from the actors? It's a bit rude, isn't it? They can see that you've written NFT, No f***ing talent.' They roared with laughter and said, 'No. It means not for this.'*

Mike Read (writer, DJ and presenter)

The Fringe

Fringe theatre is the main training ground for new directors, writers, designers, technicians and producers – all train there and many return to work in the most exciting ground-breaking venues.

Geraldine Collinge (former Programme Manager,
Battersea Arts Centre)

Actors often see 'the fringe' show as an opportunity to attract the attention of casting personnel. It certainly can be, but before taking on a commitment that will take a hefty bite out of your year and pay you in peanuts there are a number of issues you need to bear in mind.

What is 'the fringe'?

'The fringe' is a blanket term used to describe small-scale theatres and companies that operate on the margins of mainstream activity. Many are listed under 'alternative' in *Contacts*. Fringe productions are often funded by actors themselves or by private sponsorship. Fringe productions take place in studio theatres, arts centres, pub venues, open spaces, etc. There are literally hundreds of fringe companies in existence in London and in the provinces. The Edinburgh Festival bears witness to their proliferation. Many actors use the fringe to showcase their work.

Do casting directors go to fringe shows?

Yes, they do, but they are selective and more likely to be tempted by something new and interesting (an original production in a known venue on their doorstep), especially if it has attracted good reviews. *Time Out*, which offers a reliable and comprehensive guide to fringe productions, tends to be used for reviews. You will have to be very persuasive to counter a bad press.

Favourite London venues include the Bush, the Gate, the Lyric Hammersmith, the New End, the Kings Head and the Battersea Arts Centre. Casting directors like to use their time productively, so they may be less likely to be seen at a one-man show or a two-hander than a larger-cast production.

How do I know if a fringe production will be any good?

You don't, but you jolly well ought to try and find out before committing your time and energy to it. Once you have been offered a part, ask to see the script before accepting. Does it interest, stimulate or break new ground? Has the writer a track record? Does the part you are being offered suit you? How significant is it? Can you create something original and exciting in the role? Does it offer the opportunity to exhibit your talents?

Find out more about the director, his track record and his ideas about the production. Do you feel comfortable with him? Will he be enabling? Can you develop a rapport?

Don't be afraid of 'being difficult'. Nothing can be achieved by being badly directed in a poor production of a bad play with poor and inexperienced performers. Asking questions and showing genuine interest can only raise your professional profile. If the director finds it 'confrontational' it wasn't the job for you in the first place. Intelligent heart-searching actors are what the profession, at its best, is made of. If you have any doubts at all, stay away.

Who else is in the company? Established actors will often play good parts in interesting plays on the fringe. Their 'stamp of approval' should give you some grounds for confidence in the project. You will also learn from them. They will bring in upmarket contacts and may act as a lure for those elusive casting directors.

Research the artistic policy of the proposed venue. What criteria do they use for choosing plays or companies? The flash of a chequebook should not be the sole criterion for offering a company houseroom! If the previous three productions have been poor, it doesn't bode very well for the future. It certainly won't have improved the word on the street about the venue's work, which in turn will have an impact on audiences. The management will almost certainly hold reviews of back productions. Ask if you can see the file.

On a positive note, there is always brilliant work being done on the fringe by committed professionals seeking new ways of working and developing personal projects. They are the ones to look out for. They will attract everyone who is interested in good work in the theatre. Such productions are often at the cutting edge of the profession and to be seen in them can only give your career a boost.

If an actor is working, whether it's on the fringe or at the RSC, and in the meantime goes up for another audition, the chances are he will get the job. He's up, he's on a high . . . Actors always feel more confident when they are working, or have just finished a job . . . The most difficult time is when an actor has had a bad run of interviews and feels he will never work again . . .

Susanne Alvarez (Alvarez Management)

Can I afford to do a fringe show?

Fringe shows are often run on a profit-share basis. This means that the actor generally has the very last call on the company's income and can end up with nothing. Some companies pay nominal sums well below the Equity minimum; others pay only expenses. Often, even expenses have to come out of your own pocket.

During the rehearsal period, at least, you are unlikely to be able to earn money in any other way. If you are claiming income support, jobseeker's allowance or unemployment benefit you may be considered to be in breach of the basic condition of entitlement from the time you start rehearsals, regardless of whether or not you are being paid (see form UBL18 which is attached to your UB40 signing card). The Department's rule is that you must be available for and actively seeking work, and be able to prove it. This means they should be able to contact you and send you for an interview within twenty-four hours for any job you might be capable of doing. Sadly, they are unlikely to dispatch you to the RSC! If you are in any doubt about your position you should contact the office where you are claiming. But beware! The Department conducts regular random checks to detect fraud. If they consider you to be 'working' while claiming, you could be asked to repay your benefit or, at the very worst, be charged with fraud.

Should I produce my own show?

Even the most modest fringe show will cost several thousand pounds – an expensive way of attracting a handful of casting directors and agents. The economics of mounting a fringe show are shaky to say the least, and you may find it hard to pull that definitive performance out of the bag alongside checking printer's proofs, painting the backdrop and tracking down that elusive prop. That said, producing and mounting your own show can be a thrilling and life-enhancing experience in its own right. It will give you real insight into the process and the problems that other theatre companies face. Your learning curve will be in rapid ascent and you will add another useful credit to your CV. If you attract enough attention the casting directors may come too.

Putting on a show at the Edinburgh Festival Fringe

The Festival Fringe Society
180 High Street
Edinburgh EH1 1QS
Tel: 0131 226 5257
Fax: 0131 220 4205
e-mail: admin@edfringe.com
website: www.edfringe.com

The Edinburgh Festival Fringe is a brilliant shop window for actors' work. Throughout August the city teems with producers, directors, writers, talent scouts, agents and perfomers of every ilk – all keen to see as much theatre as they can. Your show will be competing with 1500 others, so make sure it stands out. Don't go with a 'so-so' show – the competition is too stiff. Good publicity is an absolute must but there is no substitute for word of mouth for getting 'bums on seats'. All the caveats set out in the previous section apply, but with a good show and a fair wind you are more likely to be 'seen' in Edinburgh than over a dingy pub in Walthamstow!

Where to begin

The first step is to register with the Fringe Society (address above) as a participant. At £12, it's an excellent investment. They will send you a pack, which tells you everything you need to know about mounting a show at the festival. It includes:

1 a venue list – giving you contact numbers and information about how to apply, a description of the venue, and information about marketing, box office and staffing
2 a fringe programme copy form – the fringe programme is the only fully comprehensive guide to what's on at the fringe and has a distribution of 300,000 copies worldwide
3 two excellent handbooks on *How to Do a Show* and *How to Sell a Show at the Edinburgh Fringe*
4 details of all the most important dates, contact details of embassies, key press contacts, a suppliers directory and information about awards.

The Fringe Society also sends out monthly bulletins containing information for performers. Read everything carefully, even if you have been to Edinburgh before. Circumstances are always changing. Every aspect of producing a show on the fringe is covered.

Some useful tips

- **Choose your venue with care** – With a good show and the right publicity it is possible to lure audiences to the hinterland of the city, but on the whole folks gravitate towards the better-known venues in the city centre. A personal recce is your best bet. I went initially with friend, tape measure and camera. If you can't do that, ask other groups about their experiences; ask venue managers for photographs, tech specs (technical specifications) and ground plans. My personal favourite is the Pleasance, a venue which operates several beautifully designed theatre spaces mainly round a convivial cobbled courtyard. Other companies swear by the Gilded Balloon, Bedlam, Venue C or the Assembly Rooms.
- **Budget carefully** – There's excellent advice on budgeting in *How to Do a Show*. Think about every possible cost you might incur and consider whether you might have to sell your body if things go horribly wrong! Your venue will probably be your biggest cost so check the 'deal'. Don't be caught out by

  1 VAT, which will be added to the service elements of your rental
  2 commission on ticket sales through the Fringe Office
  3 fees for credit/debit card sales
  4 ticket concessions.

  We seriously underestimated the concessions on the show I produced and directed with Leslie Phillips. Lots more students and senior citizens came than we expected! Budget for the worst-case scenario! Shows have been known to take no bookings at all!
- **Hire a good press agent** – It's false economy not to. It won't matter how brilliant your show is if nobody knows it's there. A friend of mine took a marvellous one-man show to the Festival a couple of years ago. He sold it round the town like a trouper but played to one man and his dog until the last week, when he was nominated as Best Actor. Suddenly his show was packed – too late, alas, to recoup!

- **Make sure your fliers and posters sell your show** – Punters wade through seas of discarded fliers. Pavements are awash. They litter café tables and cram waste-paper bins. Keep your message clear, simple, bold and memorable. Make yours the flier that shouts back from the mud; yours the poster that screams *'whatever you do, don't miss this'* from the hoardings!
- **Make your fringe programme entry a miracle of prose** – You have forty words in the fringe programme to grab the public's attention and persuade them to book your show. Make it informative, positive and eye-catching. A selling pitch! You are more likely to get an audience for a show called 'Shakespeare's Bottom' than one called 'Timetables'. Ninety-eight per cent of punters consult the fringe programme before deciding what to see!
- **Get the press in as early as you can** – The *Scotsman* reviewer sought entrance to the first preview of a show I produced and directed with Angela Pleasence. I admitted her with some reluctance, wanting the piece to find its 'mid-field rhythm' before admitting 'the press'. The show got rave reviews, was awarded a Fringe First, a nomination for Best Actress for Angela and sold out for the whole of the Festival! I won't be reluctant again!
- **Keep things simple** – There is a twenty-minute change-round between shows. Twenty minutes to get your show out and the next one in, including their respective audiences! Make sure your set is strong, quick to erect and strike, and easy to store. There's generally not much space backstage, and certainly no time for elaborate construction. It's also likely to get bashed about.
- **Time your show accurately** – *This is really important.* Punters fly round Edinburgh by taxi; they plan their theatre itinerary with military precision. They expect entries in the fringe programme to be accurate. If your show does not fit the slot you have been allocated, the venue will have no option but to ask you to make cuts – very destabilising for everyone concerned!

Whether your agenda for taking a show to the Festival is to gain experience, 'shop-window' your work, enhance your profile, make contacts or just enjoy being immersed in the world you love, the

Edinburgh Festival Fringe is the place to do it. I'd recommend it to anyone.

If you do decide to produce your own show, *The White Book* (published by Inside Communication Ltd, Bank House, 23 Coventry Road, Coventry CV1 2EW Tel: 024 76 559590 Fax: 024 76 631 1185 website: www.whitebook.co.uk) – which bills itself as the essential production directory – is an encyclopaedia of information about everything from prop hire and set constructioon to minibus hire, scene painting and marketing consultants. Very useful!

Where to Look for Work

Whether you have an agent or handle your own affairs, a key task is to glean as much information as possible about productions in preparation so that you can apply for jobs.

One source of information about forthcoming productions and casting requirements is *SBS* (Script Breakdown Services). Unfortunately, this weekly trade publication, along with other exclusive 'agent only' Internet services, is only available by subscription to bona fide agents, not to individuals. Producers, directors and casting personnel seeking artists for film, TV, theatre, light entertainment, commercials, videos and documentaries advertise their requirements there. Agents in turn submit clients for appropriate jobs.

However, there are a number of other established trade publications and casting information services you can subscribe to, which open up the casting process to the entire profession.

The Equity Job Information Service
The British Actors' Equity Association
Guild House
Upper St Martin's Lane
London WC2H 9EG
Tel: 020 7379 6000

Those who lamented the demise of Equity *Grapevine* a few years ago will be delighted with this new improved Job Information Service, launched in October 1999 as a result of a membership-wide referendum. It is available to all Equity members in full benefit.

Members are given a telephone number and a handy user guide, which enables them to access up-to-date job information cheaply and efficiently at any time of day or night. An average call lasts between four and five minutes, and at 25p per minute will cost you about £1. You'll find acting work, dancing work (ballet, contemporary dance and musicals), singing work (opera, musicals, etc.), variety, light entertainment, circus, cruises, holiday centres and non-performance creative work like theatre directing, stage management, theatre design, choreography and fight directing. A terrific range. Everything from understudy breakdowns for the National, roles in major feature films and cast changes in West End musicals to voice-over work on CD-ROM, character costume work and residencies for performers with circus skills.

In its first year of operation the service received over 19,000 calls. At the time of writing about 450 organisations have advertised vacancies there. This is an excellent service and going from strength to strength. It's well worth joining the union to gain access. One good job will pay your annual subscription!

PCR (Production and Casting Report)
PO Box 11
London N1 7JZ
Tel: 020 7566 8282
Fax: 020 7566 8284
website: www.pcrnewsletter.com

PCR was set up in 1968 by the writer, journalist and critic, the late Peter Craig-Raymond, initially to assist two daughters struggling to make contacts in the business. He was impressed with the open access to casting information in America and sought to provide a similar service in the UK. It is the longest-established casting information provider and claims a wide network of established contacts and a broad subscriber base, including actors, agents, producers, film-makers, casting directors, costumiers, caterers, scriptwriting services, etc. It claims to offer 'an accurate advanced information service and casting news for anybody and everybody who is employed on the film set, in the TV studio or the theatre'. PCR employs a small full-time team of researchers.

Its publications and services include:

Filmlog (available on the first full week of every month): a listing of films actually in production, 'almost certain' productions for forthcoming months, and useful information about studios, locations and key people, etc.

Theatre Report (available on the first full week of every month): this covers the whole regional theatre scene and other selected venues. It also incorporates 'Fringe Focus'. Detailed coverage on specific companies' regular and special casting, audition plans and programme schedules.

Who's Where: an A–Z of all contacts, updated weekly.

Who's Where in bigger print for easier reference.

Who's Where of Casting Directors: a quick reference to UK casting directors.

Who's Where USA: an A–Z of casting directors in the USA.

Castingdex: an A–Z of names and addresses of main advertising agencies (including creative and casting directors), voice-over specialists, freelance casting directors and production houses.

Information Desk: If you remember the director but not the film, the film but not the casting director, the PCR Information Desk has a successful record of tracking down information on its database. This service is available to subscribers only.

For current subscription costs contact the Subscription Office at PO Box 100, Broadstairs, Kent CT10 1UJ Tel: 01843 860885 Fax: 01843 860899. You can also subscribe via the web, access further information and request a sample copy.

ACID (Actors Casting Information Department)
Acid Publications
Suite 247
37 Store Street

London WC1E 7BS
Tel/Fax: 07050 205 206
e-mail: ACIDnews@aol.com.

ACID was set up in 1991 and is published weekly. Although it is primarily a noticeboard for actors, a number of co-operative agencies and personal managers also subscribe. It claims to provide 'a friendly and approachable service and up-to-date information about available work across the board from theatre, TV and film to murder weekends and pop promos'. *ACID* also includes two audition pieces (male and female) and information about casting personnel worldwide. Classified advertisements can be inserted at reasonable rates and casting information is accepted free of charge. Actors can also ring the *ACID* office for support and advice. *ACID* is also available via e-mail (at a slightly cheaper rate) and by fax.

Telephone for current subscription rates.

Castcall
106 Wilsden Avenue
Luton LU1 5HR
Tel: 01582 456213
Fax: 01582 480736
e-mail: admin@castcall.co.uk
website: http//www.castcall.co.uk

Castcall is a casting information provider that details casting requirements and actual breakdowns at least three times a week. It started out as a theatrical agency called Characters Agency, which now no longer exists. Frustrated by wasted time and effort following up dead-end leads, its proprietor had long pondered ways of collating and distributing casting information in a more efficient manner. The opportunity arose with the advent of premium-rate telephone lines and in 1986 Castcall was born. It describes itself as 'the actor's friend and the agent's agent', and assures its subscribers that all information is gathered first-hand, direct from the source by its proprietor – no 'rumours or gossip, may-happen or maybes'.

Because the cost of premium-rate calls is high, Castcall undertakes to keep customers' on-line time to a minimum.

Castcall is available in many ways to suit individual requirements:

Phone line: a premium-rate telephone recording on 0906 36 36 8000 (60p per minute) which details male and female roles plus the previous two updates.

Gender phone lines: a premium-rate recording which gives male roles on 0640 600 207 and female roles on 0640 600 208.

Fax subscription: dispatched three times a week for twelve weeks, with discounts on longer periods.

e-mail subscriptions: a minimum of three updates per week for the same fee as the fax service.

Postal subscription: for those who have no other means of access, Castcall offers a postal service once a week for twelve weeks.

At the time of writing Castcall is testing CastTEXT – a new service for all subscribers who will be sent text messages on their mobiles with urgent updates. There is no extra cost for this service but fax and phone subscribers will have to access the information via a premium-rate phone number. E-mail subscribers simply have access via their e-mail.

If you get a job you can put your Castcall subscription on hold (full weeks only), giving actors the opportunity to take advantage of discounts given for longer subscription periods.

Telephone for current subscription rates.

Cast-Net
99 Windmill Lane
Bushey Heath
Herts WD2 1NE
Tel/Fax: 020 8420 4209
e-mail: Cast_Net@Hotmail.com
website: www.castnet.co.uk

Cast-Net is a subscription-based 'agenting' service for all professional actors, whether you are currently represented or not. It claims to receive casting information from up to 500 productions a week, including information on all ongoing TV productions, soap castings, corporate videos, presenting jobs, radio productions, voice-overs, promotional work and major film projects in the United States requiring British actors.

There is currently a £10 enrolment fee and a two-week free trial period. Thereafter the service costs £5 a week, but actors receive one month's free subscription for every actor they recommend who becomes a paying subscriber. To maintain 'quality control' Cast-Net only accepts new subscribers by recommendation or those who have trained at an accredited British drama school, have full membership of Equity, professional publicity photographs, an entry in *Spotlight* and professional acting experience.

As Cast-Net keep a limit on the number of actors using the service you may have to wait for as long as eight weeks for a place on their list to become available. Actors leave the system for periods when they work and applicants on the waiting list take their place. You can suspend your subscription at no extra cost if you are working.

Once you have been accepted as a subscriber, you supply Cast-Net with twenty black-and-white 10 x 8 photographs and a professional CV is created for you. Cast-Net then automatically submits you for suitable jobs that come in as your agent might. Each week you are sent a Cast-Net Newsletter, an itemised report showing all the roles and productions for which you have been submitted, the number of photographs remaining on your file, the status of your subscription and a list of productions about which Cast-Net don't have enough detailed information to make targeted submissions. You can pursue these yourself. All contact regarding auditions is made directly between you (or your agent if you wish) and the appropriate casting director. If Cast-Net submits you for the same role as your agent, he will still get his commission. Cast-Net makes its money from subscriptions, not commissions.

Cast-Net will also put your CV on their website at no extra cost and for those actors with an e-mail address, Cast-Net will send details of urgent castings (commercials, etc.) and inform you that information has been sent by sending you a text message on your mobile phone.

Later this year (2001), Cast-Net plan to introduce a unique service whereby you will be able to view casting information on their website and then have your CV and photograph instantly sent by post, e-mail or fax by simply clicking a button next to the name of the production.

Profits from the service are used to fund theatre and film productions prepared to cast from actors subscribing to the service.

Contact their subscription office by telephone, fax or e-mail and they will send you a comprehensive pack about the Cast-Net service.

As actors, we have to market ourselves in the most effective ways we can. We can't just rely on our agents to promote us. We have to find other opportunities. Anyway – not everyone has an agent. Developments in technology, such as the Internet, mean that we can be represented in both sound and vision across the world. Prospective employers in New York, LA and London are able to hear your voice, watch your showreel and view your details round the clock. Technology has given us a fantastic opportunity to market ourselves creatively and cost-effectively. We can't afford to miss out and be left behind!

Gareth Hunt (actor)

e-media-c
95–96 New Bond Street
London W1S 1DB
Tel: 020 7518 1340
Fax: 020 7518 1341
e-mail: info@e-media-c.net
website: www.e-media-c.net

e-media-c is an on-line resource that was set up in 1999 to help actors, performers, agents and others to market themselves creatively to the entertainment, media and advertising industries via the Internet. The brainchild of actor Gareth Hunt, the concept was devised six years ago when he was looking through a children's encyclopaedia on CD-ROM. As he heard sound and watched moving pictures on a computer, Gareth realised how technology could benefit the industry.

With the Internet accessible all over the world, twenty-four hours a day, e-media-c claims to be the ideal venue for actors to promote themselves. Slick to look at and easy to use (Gareth reckons if he can manage to use the site – anyone can!), it presents your photos, CV, showreel and voice-over in sound and vision, giving directors and producers a more vivid understanding of you and your skills.

Their massive research engine enables casting personnel to speed up the initial casting process at the touch of a button. Everything from hair colour, height, ethnic origin, native accent and colour of eyes, to languages, accents, parachuting, Egyptian dancing and stilt-walking is categorised! Apparently one top UK advertising agency was on a tight deadline to find an actor who was also a fire-eater. e-media-c was able to come up with a shortlist of ten!

You can enter any of the following on the e-media-c site and your entry can be updated at any time.

- up to four colour or black-and-white photos
- CV
- agent's details (if relevant)
- showreel (up to ninety seconds)
- voice-over (up to sixty seconds)

You will be given a special username and password, so that you can view your entry whenever you want. Casting personnel will be able to look up your name and e-media-c number on the system at any time, anywhere in the world – cutting down costs for you and your agent.

There is a special section for drama students. Final-year students are offered the opportunity of filming an introductory piece to camera, as well as putting their details, photos and credits on to the system.

e-media-c also has separate sections for voice-overs, extras, children, presenters, dancers, light entertainers, lookalikes and singers. If you fall into two categories, you can have a double entry.

Annual subscription rates vary from £60 for an actor (£110 includes a pre-edited showreel; £150 includes an unedited showreel), £30 for a voice-over, £20 for an 'extra'. Students are free!

Contact their Performers Division by phone, e-mail or fax and they will send you a registration pack.

DannyRose.com

Avonmouth House
6 Avonmouth Street
London SE1 6NX
Tel: 020 7407 2123
Fax: 020 7357 8063
Mob: 07967 330 853
e-mail: charlied@dannyrose.com
website: www.dannyrose.com

DannyRose.com was launched at the end of August 2000. It is an on-line casting service, which markets its members throughout the Internet. The service is highly selective, only accepting registration from actors with proven professional experience and training who are fully paid-up members of British Actors' Equity. Registration on the site is entirely free, although there are plans to charge a small administration fee for actors who wish their own agents to handle enquiries.

Each actor gets his own CV page, which they can log on to and edit at any time. The actor can add showreels, a photo portfolio and update details concerning availability.

DannyRose's primary source of income is derived from finding its members work. (They work on a non-exclusive basis and charge seven and a half per cent on any work that comes through them.) Many of DannyRose's clients are corporate entities casting for training videos, PR stunts, TIE, etc.

The Stage and Television Today

The profession's weekly newspaper has a 'Situations Vacant and Auditions' section, which runs to several pages. There are generally rather more ads for singers and dancers than regional theatres looking for the cast of *Hedda Gabler* but the big West End shows usually advertise their open auditions in *The Stage* (these are valuable experiences if nothing else). Theatre and television also advertise if they have special requirements – 'Portuguese-speaking black actors sought by a Norwegian broadcasting company', I noted in one edition. A careful trawl will almost certainly throw up some interesting work with schools shows or Theatre in Education companies if you have teaching or workshop skills (see chapter 7). Fringe companies often advertise too. In the classified section you can find anything from typewriting services and accommodation to tuition in flamenco dancing and fancy-dress hire. Do check with Equity, though, before signing a six-month contract to be a singing waiter in Kowloon!

Read the body of the paper carefully and you will often glean information about forthcoming productions too.

Screen International and *Broadcast*
These are trade magazines for the film and television industry respectively and can be purchased from most good newsagents. They provide information about productions in preparation, casting personnel, directors and books that have been optioned, etc. Intelligent reading will give you avenues to research and pursue.

The Grapevine
The Grapevine – a glossy magazine – bills itself as 'the UK's leading trade magazine for the performing arts industry'. It has interviews, production news and a short 'jobs' section, which sometimes advertises for actors. The February 2001 edition advertised open auditions for three shows in Armstrong Arts touring repertory season: *Romeo and Juliet*, Sheridan's *The Critic* and Sondheim/Lapine's *Into the Woods*! It doesn't have jobs every month but it's certainly worth keeping your eye on it.

The Actors Centre Noticeboard
The Actors Centre
1A Tower Street
London WC2H 9NP
Tel: (general enquiries) 020 7240 3940

If you are an Actors Centre Member (Equity membership and a modest subscription secures your annual membership to this training base for professional performers – see chapter 8) you will have access to the members' noticeboard. All ads are carefully vetted and range from modestly paid film-school training films and low-budget movies to more mainstream work in theatre and TV. Many of the Actors Centre tutors work in the profession and often turn to the 2000-strong membership when they are casting.

Off Stage Theatre and Film Bookshop
37 Chalk Farm Road
London NW1 8AJ
Tel: 020 7485 4996

There is a noticeboard in the front of the shop which sometimes advertises jobs, singing teachers, voice coaches, etc., so it's certainly worth popping in if you are in the area.

Mailing lists of regional theatres
Any theatre will put you on their audience mailing list free of charge if you ask them. This will give you early information about productions in the pipeline so you will have time to investigate whether there are any suitable parts for you. *French's Guide to Selecting Plays*, which lists and describes all the plays published by Samuel French, should be your first port of call (see page 83).

British Film Institute Library
21 Stephen Street
London W1T 1LN
Tel: 020 7255 1444

e-mail: library@bfi.org.uk

Membership of the British Film Institute library will give you access to some casting information sheets like *PCR*, *Film Log*, *Film News* and other useful trade publications mentioned in this chapter. Membership might save you money in the long run. An annual pass costs £33, with concessionary rates for the unemployed, etc., and special day passes currently cost £6.

5 Demonstrating your Wares

It's a jungle out there. If you think you're good, you have to think, 'They'll be lucky to get me.' Which is the same technique that salesmen have to learn. When I sold encyclopaedias in Hollywood, the company taught me one very important thing, which I never forgot. It's this. If you fail to make a sale in one house, you have to leave that house thinking, 'Aren't they unlucky to have passed up this wonderful opportunity!' If you leave thinking, 'I failed. I didn't make my pitch,' you carry that failure around with you and don't make a sale next door either.

David Benedictus (actor and novelist)

The Audition

An audition is a demonstration of what you have to sell as a performer. The actor hopes the audition will be the gateway to employment. The director hopes to find the best person for the part. If you get called to audition it's generally because you have been shortlisted from a considerable number of applicants on the basis of your CV and photograph. The director will have a fairly clear idea what he is looking for and whether your experience and physical appearance fall within these parameters.

He may only be seeing half a dozen people for the part, so once you have been invited to audition you know you are already a strong contender. Your sales package has got you through the door. Now you must present yourself and your talents in the best possible light. You need to show that you are talented, co-operative, intelligent, flexible and directable, and that you are right for this particular part. Even if the director makes another choice, you must make certain you are remembered for next time.

At the end of the audition process the director needs to feel that he has made the best possible choice and assembled a company of actors who will work together compatibly and creatively. The late Lindsay Anderson used to say that seventy-five per cent of a director's job was done if he got the casting right. Get it wrong and the whole production is at risk. It is quite likely that the director is feeling as nervous as you are!

The thing that you fear most when you are auditioning is that somebody will come in and be quite dull in the audition but actually, given the right opportunity, they will have some sort of extraordinary blossoming which will come through rehearsal and imagination ... that's why I often just enjoy meeting people. I often go on my hunches.

Jude Kelly (Artistic Director, West Yorkshire Playhouse)

Choosing text for theatre auditions

I was summoned to audition for Joan Littlewood at Theatre Workshop. I was a young actor and very excited. I had written to her. It was the Theatre Royal, Stratford East. When I arrived at the theatre, Joan wasn't there so I found myself auditioning for Gerry Raffles. When I was up on stage Gerry said, 'Ah, Carl, what would you like to do for us?' I said, 'I can do Jimmy Porter – Look Back in Anger ...' 'Christ,' he said, 'I don't want that!' 'Brutus – Friends, Romans and Countrymen ... ?' 'Oh fuckin' 'ell ... I don't want any Shakespeare! That's boring.' 'Um ... Bit of The Caretaker – Harold P ... ?' 'Can't stand him!' I said, 'That's it. You've got my three pieces.' He said, 'What's your dad like ... ?' I said, 'He's Welsh ... Welsh Italian.' So I did an improvisation of my dad ... My dad used to do a lot of 'bloodying' amd 'buggering', so I 'bloodied' and 'buggered' around the stage, improvising my dad and Gerry just fell about laughing ... When I'd finished he said, 'Do you want to be in

the next show?' Do I ... Did I want to be in the next show!?
The late Carl Forgione (actor)

For a theatre audition you may be asked for a couple of 'contrasting pieces'. 'Something classical and something modern' seems to be a general request, although one of my students was recalled three times in the space of two weeks and required to perform eight pieces. Fortunately she had an extensive repertoire. Her experience is the exception rather than the rule, but it is best to be on the safe side.

Every three years Samuel French publish an extremely useful book called *The Guide to Selecting Plays for Performance*, which is an update of their earlier edition and is a catalogue of all the plays they sell. Between times they publish a biannual supplement (spring and autumn) called *The Supplement*, which gives details of all new releases. *The Guide* and *The Supplement* are available in French's Theatre Bookshop (52 Fitzroy Street, London W1T 5JR Tel: 020 7387 9373). *The Supplement* will be sent to you free of charge if you are on Samuel French's mailing list or the latest edition can be downloaded from their website (www.samuelfrench-london.co.uk). Titles in *The Guide* are arranged according to the number of characters and according to period and/or type of play (Classics, Biblical, Late-Victorian, Plays with Courtroom Scenes, Military Plays, Irish/Scots/Welsh plays and so on) and it is therefore extremely useful to actors looking for appropriate audition pieces and identifying parts that they might want to play. It has a cast breakdown for each play giving the male/female ratio, together with a note of any ethnic characters involved.

If, for instance, you discover Pitlochry is putting on Tom Stoppard's *Travesties*, it is fairly easy to discover a little of what it's all about and whether there might be anything in it for you. The entry reads:

Travesties. Play, Tom Stoppard

M5 (20s–middle-age, 60s) F3 (young, 40s) A library, a drawing room.

James Joyce, running a Swiss theatrical company, invites Henry Carr to play in Oscar Wilde's *The Importance of Being Earnest.* Carr agrees and scores a success, but later there is a dispute over Carr's claim for reimbursement of the cost of clothing bought for his role. The author uses this factual framework on which to build an extravaganza of political history, literary pastiche and Wildean parody, even song and dance, introducing Dadaist Tristan Tzara and Lenin and his wife. Period 1918.

Let's assume you are an Irish actor in your mid-twenties. This immediately puts you in the running for playing James Joyce. Read the play. It's a fascinating piece of work and in any event will be an interesting addition to your repertoire. The entry indicates that it is a play about a real character and based on a true story, so research about Joyce's physical appearance, his life and work will be important. Who was Henry Carr? Find out! Read *The Importance of Being Earnest.* It is clearly relevant. Armed with information about the character, an understanding of the play and the knowledge that you have the right physical and geographical credentials, you are now in a good position to target your application and handle the interview/audition intelligently should it come your way. Look at James Joyce's writing. Can you cull a suitable audition piece from that? Perhaps a couple of minutes from *A Portrait of the Artist as a Young Man,* Joyce's autobiographical novel? It would certainly be an interesting choice and show the director that you had done your homework!

The Supplement gives you even more help. It gives potted descriptions of the characters too.

Chasing the Moment by Jack Shepherd

M4 F2 A basement club

This could be the last gig for Les Padmore and his jazz band. Wes, the founder of the club, is on life support in hospital and there are major rifts between members of the band, rifts which become more and more obvious and painful as the night progresses. Les looks back to a golden age of jazz and is highly suspicious of the younger, more progressive members of the band; Tony, the black drummer, seeks acceptance from his fundamentalist father and fails yet again to receive it; Harry, booze-sodden and high on drugs, is desperate for money for his next fix, and young Joe tries to find solace with Tony's unwilling sister Sharon: all are seeking, in the teamwork and harmony of the music, a balance to the chaos of their lives. Poignant, witty and so real you can smell the cigarette smoke and stale beer, this is a gritty and haunting play full of insights and wry philosophy.

Les: cynical, nostalgic; middle-aged. Tony: intelligent, level-headed, black; young. Joe: sex-mad, cool, young. Joanne: highly strung, emotional, young. Sharon: long-suffering, articulate, black, young. Harry: spaced-out, bad-tempered, old.

There is no doubt that the more audition pieces you have in your repertoire, the more likely you are to be able to pull out something appropriate as required. If you are auditioning for a trousers-round-your-ankles farce, the sleepwalking scene from *Macbeth* will probably not impress. A witty, middle-class monologue from Ayckbourn may not give you the edge in an audition for Berkoff's *East*. Common sense really. Develop a range of contrasting pieces that show your talent off to its best advantage and suit the occasion. A Piece For All Seasons. Even if you never need all of them, the process of doing the work is important in itself, and confidence-building.

A library of play texts is a must for every actor. A Complete Shakespeare, Shaw, Chekhov, Ibsen, Molière, plays by contemporary writers, etc. should be found on every actor's bookshelf. I find charity shops, market stalls and second-hand bookshops an invaluable source. New books are expensive. For a few pounds I have frequently acquired five or six useful texts to add to my collection. Keep your eyes open when you go to the theatre and make a note of any part you think might suit you.

Remember that play texts are not the only source of suitable audition material. You have the whole of literature at your disposal. A favourite character from Dickens, Trollope or Balzac might fit the bill. Films and TV are rich territory too. Transcribe speeches off your video. Police series often conclude with a 'why I did it' or a 'what makes her tick' speech which can be original and useful. I have seen actors perform Victoria Wood and Joyce Grenfell sketches, assume the mantle of prosecuting council from a transcript of the trial of *Lady Chatterley's Lover* and audition very effectively with a Robert Burns poem. Richard Pasco told me that one actor finally got into the RSC after unsuccessful attempts by standing on his head and reciting 'You are old, Father William . . .' Many film scripts are in print. Finally, some of the most interesting audition pieces I have seen have been written by actors themselves. If you have that kind of talent, it will also give you something to talk about in the subsequent interview.

There are also a number of audition books on the market containing classical and modern monologues for men and women. (see bibliography). These will introduce you to plays you may not have come across. The monologues are usually prefixed with a brief but not entirely illuminating introduction.

Sasha. Aged 20. She is the daughter of one of Ivanov's neighbours. He is an ageing malcontent and she is in love with him . . .

Jean, early 30s, tries to explain to her white husband why she ran off with a black scuba diver . . .

Felicity, Countess of Marshwood, knows that her son Nigel is engaged to a film star and is not altogether pleased with the idea. She has been handed the telephone, with the information that Nigel is on the other end of the line . . .

An audition book will give you some idea of monologues that might suit you. Don't fillet a monologue from an audition book without reading the play first. The introductions tell you very little about the style and content of the play, and you could come horribly unstuck. The director may ask more about the character and his/her relationships. Chekhov's *Ivanov* might be his favourite play. You certainly won't make a good impression by saying, 'I don't know. I found the piece in an audition book...' so beware of short cuts. The disadvantage of trawling through any recently published audition book, of course, is that every actor and his dog are probably doing the same thing. After a very tiring day, and feeling less than charitable, a director may not react kindly to the umpteenth Viola launching into the umpteenth, 'I left no ring with her, what means this lady...'

I had been an actor for quite some time before I had my first audition at the National, which was a really awful experience. I remember my father, who was an actor [Sir Cedric Hardwicke], saying to me, 'Never ever do the well-known pieces. If Henry Irving walked on the stage and did a piece from Hamlet, *I would ignore him.' This was one of the few pieces of advice he ever gave me that I really took on board. Consequently I rummaged around in the depths of* Henry VI Part III *for something to do from that. There is a wonderful scene in* Henry VI *that's known as 'the triptych scene'. Really obscure. I thought, 'Nobody's going to do that.' I was due to audition for the National Theatre Directors, who were Sir Laurence Olivier, John Dexter, Bill Gaskell, etc. at some theatre in the West End. It was all fairly intimidating for a young actor. In the wings of the theatre there were two benches with a row of actors waiting to audition. It was like being in a doctor's waiting room and you could hear what was going on on stage ... well, the actor in front of me was called and blow me down if he didn't do exactly the same speech. Before I could make my getaway the stage manager shouted, 'Mr Hardwicke, please. Sir Laurence is waiting ...' I was so nonplussed, I had got up to leave! I didn't, as it happened, get into the company at that point but I was later invited to join without having to do a second audition.*

Edward Hardwicke (actor)

John Harrison maintains he doesn't care how often he hears 'To be, or not to be . . .', he can spot the next Derek Jacobi from fifty paces. He's right, of course. Talent will shine 'like a good deed in a naughty world' through a rendition of the telephone directory.

> *In my extreme youth my audition pieces used to be Rosalind from* As You Like It *and Curly's wife in* Of Mice and Men, *both extraordinarily inappropriate; I never got to play either part, but I did quite often get the job!*
>
> Prunella Scales (actor)

Sometimes directors 'know' the minute an actor walks through the door. In any event an original audition piece is bound to attract attention and stimulate enquiry. I always sit up when an actor does a piece I haven't heard before.

Preparing your audition piece

Before learning your piece, find out everything you possibly can about the play and the character. The play text will be littered with clues: age, class, background, period, etc. What are the dominant conventions operating in the play? Where does the play fall in the canon of theatre history? What does it require stylistically? The pace and cadence of the language will help you too. Is it clipped and brisk; disjointed and hesitant; florid and luxurious? What do other characters say about the character? Where does the scene take place? Where has he come from? What does he do? Where is he heading? What does he want? What is he trying to communicate? What are his relationships with other characters? Is there anything in your emotional repertoire that will inform the work?

In one of my classes at the Actors Centre a young woman came with a piece from *Antigone* by Jean Anouilh to work on. The play is based on the Greek tragedy in which Antigone tries to bury her brother's corpse, against the diktat of her uncle, Creon. Her work was obviously blocked somewhere. She couldn't remember the lines . . . she stumbled, foundered. It was very painful to watch. After some gentle unpicking, it was revealed that her brother in real life had committed suicide, and being unable to come to terms with his death she had not been able to visit the grave. No wonder she was having problems. Yet what was blocking her work was actually the emotional experience she needed to inform the part. Once she was able to acknowledge and take hold of this painful experience it became a powerful tool in her interpretation of the role.

Take the improbable line '*I, who was young and beautiful, am ironing socks.*'

What does it tell us? A woman, no longer in her prime, feels the loss of youth and beauty, and is reduced to a futile domestic chore: ironing socks. What could be more useless? Where is she? It is likely that she is in her own home. She irons as she speaks. Why would she iron socks? Is this her role in life? Perhaps she wishes to be perceived as a caring wife and mother. We assume she is a married lady. These are not her socks. Her husband's socks perhaps? Her son's? Is she lonely, bored, with nothing better to do? Is she happy? The stark comparison she makes between her past and present makes it seem unlikely. How old is she? We don't know precisely, but we sense she is hankering after a not-too-distant past. A past that is lost and gone. This is not social realism. But we are in the present. Irons have been invented. Men wear socks. The language is measured and stylised. It has an internalised, reflective quality. A soliloquy perhaps? It *feels* middle-class. Why? Maybe the careful grammatical use of 'I'? Would the 'upper classes' be seen dead at the ironing board, let alone putting creases in a pair of socks? We are steeped in assumptions. A 'working-class' version of the same sentiments might look rather more like this:

'*I was a cracker when I was young. Now look at me. Ironing bleeding socks.*'

Thus we can wrest an enormous amount of information from a very small amount of text with minimum knowledge of its context.

Once you have done your homework, apply it to the text. If you understand the thought processes of the character, the text will be much easier to learn. When you have done everything you can on your own, *get some help*. Unless you have considerable experience, I would strongly advise you not to 'go it alone'. The gyrating monster grimacing at you from your bedroom mirror will give you no clues. You can't watch yourself being your character with any degree of objectivity. It's the internal landscape you need to get right. You can't see that in a mirror. Nor will your voice on audio cassette be much good for anything except perhaps learning your lines in the car. Many actors find listening to themselves very destructive. Attempts to reproduce an inflexion that 'sounds good' often destroys the truthful impulse that created it.

Endless work and repetition sometimes makes a piece feel as if it is set in concrete. Sometimes it's useful to try a fresh approach. Delivering it laughing or at speed or with a Birmingham accent or with a stutter can often reinvigorate it and help you look at it in a new light. You will find lines will be delivered in wholly unexpected ways.

Coaches

You will find a number of experienced and well-respected acting coaches under the Drama Training, Schools and Coaches section of *Contacts*. If you are a member of the Actors Centre (see chapter 9) they offer very modestly priced audition workshops and private sessions with well-known actors and directors. You have to be a member of Actors' Equity to join. The classified advertisements in *The Stage* are full of people offering classes too. A couple of hours' work on your piece with support and advice from a qualified outside eye will make all the difference. Apart from anything else, working on text with an imaginative and stimulating director will provide a focus for your work. Book a class and you will have to knock that piece into a reasonable shape for public consumption.

Private classes can be expensive, on average around £30 per hour, so make sure you choose a coach with a good reputation and strong paper qualifications or a body of experience as a teacher or director. Ask other actors whom they would recommend. The Actors Centre holds a list of tutors whose work they would endorse. Once you have found a teacher who really enables your work, stretches your talent and builds your confidence, you will never want to let him go. I know actors who have been going to the same drama coach for years.

If you can't afford private coaching, at the very least perform your pieces for a fellow actor. Persuade him to stand in for the other characters in your scene so that you can re-create the dynamic of action and reaction more readily in the audition situation.

What should I wear for an audition?

Terry Gilliam's first film after Monty Python *was* Jabberwocky *and they wanted a very big woman who was terrifically ugly ... Another audition at short notice. In the first instance I was to go along and see the casting director, Irene Lamb, at her home in Walton Street. Orange does not suit me so I decided to wear a tight orange scarf round my neck to make my double chin look bigger ... I knew the colour would look hideous ... and glasses. I wanted Billy Bunter/ Miss Piggy kind of glasses so I went to my local optician, who had what I wanted, but with a strong prescription lens through which I could not see, or at least very dimly! I scraped my hair back, wore a voluminous dress and arrived at the audition in the glasses – I saw a vague haze open the door ... I could not see Irene go down the corridor, I could not focus on her and I don't know what I would have done if they'd asked me to read a script. I did get the job but I wouldn't do that now. I dress 'in the manner of ...' I wouldn't be so specific. I think casting directors should have more imagination!*

Annette Badland (actor)

The most important thing is to be comfortable. You won't do your best work unless you feel relaxed and confident. Clothes that make you feel less like yourself, clothes you have never worn before or are unlikely to wear again except at a fancy-dress ball, are not a good idea. If you *feel* your best, you will have a good chance of *giving* your best. Shoes, in particular, should be comfortable and not clatter distractingly as you move about. Aim for the middle ground. Choose clothing that gives a hint of the character but makes you feel serene and happy as well. You wouldn't be auditioning for the part if you were a million miles from what the director had in mind.

There is, of course, an ongoing debate among actors about the advisability of *dressing for the part*. We all know apocryphal stories about the actor who arrives at the audition in motorbike helmet, leather gear and gauntlets, claiming he has left his non-existent Harley on the forecourt, and gets cast before he has had a chance to sit down. It does happen and actors have got work this way. However, taken to extremes, you could find yourself auditioning in full Viking battle dress or a crinoline!

> *We were up in Glasgow auditioning with the Scottish Youth Theatre for my musical,* What a Way to Run a Revolution. *The auditions were open to anyone who wanted to come and a local acting school brought a whole series of little girls from this school aged about eleven or twelve. The teacher who had been coaching them in audition technique had obviously got her ideas from old Carmen Miranda films because these little things would arrive dressed provocatively in a swimsuit with a circlet of fruit around their waists and on one occasion, a little girl having done her number, which was toothsomely horrible, sat in the lap of the musical director and fed him with one of her bananas! Although I had great difficulty keeping a straight face, I was also filled with a sense of deep tragedy, because if they had any talent it would have been totally obfuscated by the disastrous audition technique that had been foisted on them by a failed and out-of-date teacher. The musical was about a mining dispute in the Depression, so their outfits could hardly have been less appropriate!*
>
> David Benedictus (actor and novelist)

If you are auditioning for the part of a high-class hooker, it makes sense to jettison your cuddly cardigan in favour of something more glamorous. On the other hand there is no point in trying to second-guess the director's vision. The high-class hooker in his production might wear Jaeger!

Fear is the enemy

The telephone rings. An audition next Tuesday? This could be the job that changes your name from Hermione Jobbing-Theatrical to Hermione Big-Star. The carrot dangles. Suddenly your relaxed and carefree mood turns to panic. Fear can be so disabling – it is the rock on which so many of us stumble. Nothing is more fearful than fear itself – it paralyses us. So how can we avoid its destructive and enervating effects?

Confront your fear. Is it the fear of failure? Be positive. Failure can be your friend. We can analyse it and learn from it. In today's failure are the seeds of tomorrow's success. Fear of being rejected? Some actors seem to set themselves up for rejection. 'I'm awfully sorry,' you hear them mumble, 'I haven't had time to read the play ...' or 'I've never really seen myself playing sexy parts ...' or 'I didn't have time to get to the library for the text...'

Any director will tell you that casting often hinges on the colour of your hair or your height in relation to the leading man. It is an actor's stock-in-trade to have his hopes raised over and over again, only to have them dashed to the ground. If you take every rejection personally, your self-esteem will soon hit rock bottom. It is a fact of life that you won't be right for every audition you go up for. An actor friend of mine reckons he gets one in six.

> *Often in the audition process you meet actors and think, 'God, you're good ... you're really good ...' but you can't really give them anything because they're just not right for the part you're seeing them for. It's really hard to make actors understand that you're not turning them down because they're less good than somebody else, you're turning them down because they're not right in some way. Actors get very upset about this but if you ask an actor, 'What did you think of such and such a production?' they'll often say, 'So and so was completely wrong for that part' ...!*
>
> Jude Kelly (Artistic Director, West Yorkshire Playhouse)

Try to keep things in proportion. Does it *really* matter if you get this job? What's the very worst thing that can happen if you don't? Of course it feels important but you were managing perfectly well before the telephone rang. Suddenly you are a nervous wreck. It doesn't make a lot of sense, does it? Half the world is starving for want of a handful of rice and you are getting into a state about a commercial for Ryvita. Think of the good things in your life – your home, your partner and your children. You will fare far better in an audition if you have a grounded sense of well-being. When all is said and done, family and friends will still be there long after this job has come, gone and been forgotten.

Live in the present. Speculating about success or failure is corrosive and distracting. You have a lot of work to do before next Tuesday. Structure the days between now and then with creative activities. Polish up your sight-reading technique or a couple of suitable audition pieces. Go to the gym – good health, strength and stamina are crucial resources and will do wonders for your self-esteem. Keep busy. Don't give yourself time to fret. Deserve success.

The dreaded hour!

Try to avoid last-minute panics by arriving good and early at your audition. When I was a performer I always had a little bag packed with everything I needed – an A–Z with precise instructions about my route and destination; a bag of small change for parking meters; hairbrush and make-up; tissues and a spare pair of tights. It gave me confidence that I had done everything I possibly could to prepare myself. Even if you don't go this far, it is useful to prepare a few things in advance so you can leave the house in a calm and confident frame of mind. Give yourself a good half-hour longer than the maximum time you think you need to get there to obviate cardiac arrest at the first sign of a broken traffic light or cancelled train!

Take with you:

- Details of travel arrangements. Being late or getting lost is not a good start.
- Notes your agent has given you about the part you are up for, the company, the director, etc. Refresh your memory while you are travelling or waiting.
- Typed copies of your audition pieces headed with your name, the name of the play, the playwright and your character. Be prepared to leave it behind. It will be a useful *aide-mémoire* at the end of a long day.
- A spare CV and photograph. Your showreel. A recent photographic contact sheet and your portfolio.
- Your agent's telephone number (if it is not already written on your heart), so you can give feedback on how you think it went.
- Your diary – just in case you're offered the part on the spot. You certainly don't want to be caught short if the director says, 'What are you doing in the first week of June? Are you free?' Consult your diary carefully. It looks more professional than letting out a wild whoop and saying, 'Nothing at all. I'm actually free for the rest of my life!'

Body language in interviews

One of the most useful exercises we do in the Actors Centre workshops is to role-play the interview process. It tells both observers and participants a great deal about the simple traps we fall into in the interview situation – especially when we are nervous!

Body language is a complex and fascinating subject. Many excellent books have been written about it and we can only scratch the surface here. Non-verbal communication of our inner feelings can often be more indicative of them than any words. The flutter of eyelashes, a raised eyebrow, the wringing of hands, a pointing finger, a clenched fist, open, welcoming arms: all have unspoken meanings in our culture that each of us can read and understand. Our bodies can exhibit anything from disapproval and disagreement to sincerity and deceit.

This is a typical role-play exercise:

Our guinea pig, a woman (let us call her **A**) is dispatched to the outside corridor. She exits with jaunty steps – this is, after all, only an exercise. She will show us how it is done! We begin with the premise that her agent has given her a limited amount of information about the role she is auditioning for and she knows whether the interview is for theatre, TV or film. She has not seen a script. A desk and chairs are set out – two chairs behind and one in front. A couple of actors assume the role of casting personnel (they both serve an identical function so let us call them **B**). We do all we can to simulate the real-life situation. While **A** waits outside in the corridor, the group discusses how the interview should be conducted. We exchange experiences. Settle on questions that **B** can ask:

What have you been doing lately?
Tell me a little bit about yourself?
What makes you think you are right for this part?
There doesn't seem to be a great deal of television on your CV, does there?

Sound familiar? It is a typical selection of questions actors learn to expect.

We leave **A** to 'sweat it out' for a few minutes, then she is invited in. The observers have been instructed to watch **A**'s entrance, her handshake, her body language – to be analytical about the way she sells her product. How will she conduct herself? What impression will she make?

She enters. She is nervous. Her CV and photograph are on the desk. Her wait in the corridor has had a sobering effect, no doubt triggering memories of real experiences. She is no longer jaunty. Her steps are small. In fact, she seems smaller altogether. She hesitates before offering her hand, which she extends, palm upward in classic supplication. **B** shakes it firmly – his palm securely on top. The terms of reference of this encounter have already been set. Unlike **A**, **B** appears to have grown larger. He moves with confident grace and gestures **A** to sit. The dynamic of the situation is archetypal. **B** is in control of his territory – our simulated office space. He leans forward confidently on the desk or tips backwards on his chair, both hands clasped supportively behind his head. He makes strong eye contact.

A sits away from the desk, maximising the acreage of space between them. Her arms are crossed and defensive, or clenched with white knuckles on the arms of the chair. Sometimes they are in the position of prayer. Alternatively, a hand flies to her face, partially covering her mouth as she speaks. Her ankles are crossed and locked, her chin is lowered and defensive. Everything about her is closed, shut down. Perhaps **A** leans forward, anxiously trying to get her message across while **B** cups his chin between thumb and forefinger, fingers curled under his mouth, critically evaluating the impact. Their bodies are both fascinating hieroglyphics of an inner state.

B launches into the first stages of the interview with a predictable opening gambit. 'Tell me a little bit about yourself.' We see **A**'s brain go into overdrive. What on earth does **B** want to know? Does he want to know about her scuba-diving holiday off Paxos, the birth of her twins or something about that definitive TV cameo – sadly lost on the cutting-room floor? There is nothing more likely to rivet your tongue to your palette or erase all memory of recent events.

Once the interview is under way I ask the participants to 'freeze' and for the observers to analyse what they see. It's not difficult to read the signs. The scene we are watching might be of a teacher and pupil, a parent and child or a soldier and commanding officer. **B** looks superior, in authority, happy and confident in his space. **A** looks subordinate, the supplicant, her desperation about 'getting the job' writ large on every line of her body. There is a murmur of recognition from the group.

It has been very useful to see what we do wrong, but how can we put it right? How can we avoid re-creating these archetypal relationships in the interview situation and present ourselves in a better light?

I ask **A** to imagine that **B**, despite his confident body language, is nervous. **B** readily admits he didn't know what to ask. Directors rarely have training in interview technique! He likes **A**'s photograph and CV. She has the right skills and experience. She is one of a small handful of actors he will interview this morning. It is just as important to **B** to find the right actor for the job as it is for **A** to land it. He feels at risk. He must somehow unlock the talent of a nervous interviewee. ('I had terrible stage fright and it wasn't based on whether I'd be good or not, it was based on what people would think of me,' confessed Shirley Maclaine in her autobiography *Out on a Limb*. What bells it rings!) I ask **A** to take responsibility for making **B** feel at ease. I ask her to empathise with **B**'s difficulty. Give him a helping hand. Casting is a dicey business. He has a lot at stake. **A** must help him make up his mind – preferably in her favour. We agree to rerun the interview.

The impact is spectacular. Instead of focusing on her own fear – fear of being rejected, fear of being judged – **A** concentrates instead on **B**'s anxieties about casting this play. **A** rearranges her mindset in the corridor and concentrates on putting those poor people at their ease. This act of generosity distracts her attention from her own problems. Instead of looking 'in', she is looking 'out'. This time she enters the room with a confident stride, takes the initiative with a friendly handshake, then sits with steady assurance. Her smile is open and infectious. Her back is straight. Her shoulders are square. Her feet are firmly planted on the floor just a few inches apart. The whole impression is of openness and accessibility. As the interview proceeds **B** begins to respond. **A** feels good to have around. He likes her. His head tilts in eloquent interest. He smiles receptively. **A**'s confidence is fed. She is enabled by **B**'s relaxed engagement. This, in turn, facilitates a relationship of fair and equal exchange. **A** and **B** are both aware that each has something valuable to offer the other. It is a much more accurate reflection of the dynamics of the situation than the superior/subordinate relationship our guinea pigs enacted earlier.

> *The relationship between the actor and director isn't a 'master/ servant' relationship; it's a relationship of equals. Actors must learn never to say, 'I've worked for so-and-so.' 'I've worked with so-and- so' is the way we have to think.*
>
> Edward Hardwicke (actor)

I don't know whether this story is apocryphal or true but it's a wonderful story ... Terry Hands, Trevor Nunn and John Barton were auditioning for a season at Stratford when a tall bloke, a Peter Cook-type wearing a hat and long mac, came in. The stage manager announced his name but nobody knew who he was. 'Tell us a bit about yourself,' one of them asked. 'No,' he replied, 'first of all, let me ask you a few questions. You, for instance,' he said, pointing at John Barton, 'What have you done?' 'Well,' said John Barton, 'I've been directing for the Royal Shakespeare Company for many years and I ...' 'Any good? Are you any good? Many successes?' And he grilled them all like this for a while. When he had finished they ventured, 'Would you like to audition for us now?' 'No,' he replied, fixing them with a steely glare, 'I don't think so.' And he walked off! Trevor Nunn shouted, 'Stop him!' The stage manager went after him but he had disappeared. They swear that they would have given him the job, but they never did find out who it was.

Bill Homewood (actor, director)

'Cold-reading'

In many audition situations you will be asked to sight-read from a text. This is called 'cold-reading'.

'She's a myopic campanologist from Hull,' mutters the director, handing you a page of script that you've never seen in your life before. He has offered you 'the comfy chair' and you have sunk so low into its foam that your bottom hits the floor. He, on the other hand, sits proud and tall on his office chrome behind a vast desk. Distance does not lend enchantment. The page quivers between your fingers. He tries to tell you a little more about the character, but his meaning eludes you. What on earth is a campanologist? Anyway, you are trying to get a sneak preview of the text before the dreadful moment of delivery is upon you. It is a blur. He smiles. You freeze. 'Would you like to read it for me?' he asks. You manage glassy-eyed acquiescence. Your throat tightens, your body language, not aided by the 'comfy chair', is foetal, the acid bile of fear rises in your throat and the script starts to do a rumba of its own volition. Then, with the wonderfully expressive top of your head pointing in his general direction, you stumble uncomprehendingly through the text, feeling like a six-year-old former self taking a first shot at Janet and John in front of Class 2B. You wish, with every fibre of your being, that you'd taken that apprenticeship with your Uncle Percy's upholstery firm – anything, anything but be an actor.

Let's rewind the scene, back to the beginning . . .

'She's a myopic campanologist from Hull,' mutters the director, handing you a page of script that you've never seen in your life before . . . 'Can you tell me a little more about how you see the character?' you ask steadily. He does. Genuine interest in the part and the production focuses your attention on something other than your fear. (Remember, he has spouted the information about the script and the characters so many times, he probably knows it off by heart. 'I know you must have been through this a thousand times but it would be really helpful if . . .' might endear you to him.) If there are other people at your audition, try to involve them too. The writer, the producer might be present and will almost certainly have a say in the casting process.

You listen carefully to what the director has to say, taking on board the key points. You ask if you can have five minutes to read the text. The director wants to see you at your best. What helps you helps him, so your request shouldn't be a problem. If he refuses, it is probably because he is time-constrained, not because he is trying to be difficult. You read the text carefully and make a few simple decisions. If you are dispatched to the corridor it will be focusing to read the text aloud. When we are stressed we often 'read' but don't 'see'. The director will have given you some helpful clues about the character and wants to see how you respond to his suggestions. He needs to know you are directable. He won't be looking for a polished performance. That's what rehearsals are for. A flash of talent and integrity will sing out through any fumbled or mispronounced words. If you can deliver that, it will be enough.

Some useful tips:

- You don't have to read from the depths of your low-level chair. You won't do your best work with your diaphragm under your tonsils. The director is unlikely to have any objection if you stand or move a chair into an appropriate position. And the act of 'setting the scene', however simply, will give you a sense of confidence and control. It will also give you a little time to compose yourself.
- Well-known actors often refuse to audition or 'read' for a part, expecting to be offered work on the basis of their reputations. Never, ever say, 'I don't do readings', however grand and famous you become. Arrogance impresses nobody. 'Big ego, small talent' as the saying goes.

> *I was auditioning for Peter Ustinov some time in the late 1970s. I can't remember the name of the play but it was a comedy. I was feeling rather grand and told him I wasn't going to read. 'Come, come,' said Peter, 'we all have to do it!' Reluctantly, and in a foul temper, I really went for it – gave it all I'd got. After a while I became aware of chuckling from the stalls. 'T. P.,' he said, 'I think you've just disproved your point!'*
>
> T. P. McKenna (actor)

- Don't plough straight into the reading. Take your time. Create the character's world in your imagination before you begin – the scenery, the costumes, the weather, the other characters in the scene, etc. – anything and everything that might help you step seamlessly into it.
- Be bold! Take the character by the horns and ride it. The director will see more of your potential from a brave stab than from any tentative mumblings. Even if he doesn't think you are right for this job, with a bit of luck he will remember your talent and your courage next time he's casting.
- If you make a start but feel you could do better, stop immediately and say so. There is no director in the world who wouldn't prefer you to do that than blunder on! 'Do you mind if I start again? It isn't coming out quite as I intended' will show you are in control

of your work and conscientiously self-critical.

- You can't do a Hull accent? Don't worry about it. Colour the text with your 'all-purpose northern' and draw the director's attention to the legend on your CV that you have 'a good ear for accents'. If he wants you for your talent and other qualities, putting a Hull accent in place is a technical matter to be addressed in rehearsal. Don't let it be a problem that trips you up at the audition stage. A dialect coach or a tape from a sound archive will soon solve the problem.
- Cherish the pauses. A good actor can do more with a look than with a paragraph. The pause after a line like 'For Christ's sake . . .' might be filled with, 'You have hurt me more than I can say, and I will never, never forgive you.' A pause can be mighty powerful in the right hands!
- This is not a reading test. If you trip or fumble over a word, don't stop and say sorry – it destroys the illusion. If necessary, correct yourself in character and carry on. Similarly, if you come across a word or phrase you don't understand, deliver it with conviction.
- Keep your place by running your thumb slowly down the left margin of the text as you read. Take it slowly. Ingest a few words, invest them with the character's thoughts and feelings, *look up* and deliver them. Repeat the process. No good will come of performing to the carpet. The director must see the work in your face. If you do lose your place, don't panic. Stay in character. Take your time. You will find the missing line somewhere in the general vicinity of your thumb.
- Some directors enjoy reading with you. This breed will be looking for eye contact. Make sure you 'play the scene' with them. They can't watch you while they are reading their part, but they *can* make judgements on the way you handle pauses and reactions. Make sure you give them the chance.

My father used to say, 'A penny-worth of implication is worth a pound of explicit statement.'

Edward Hardwicke (actor)

- Don't obscure your work with hair, hats or spectacles. If you do need to wear glasses, wear ones without heavy frames.
- Deliver the piece 'out front'. The director is no more interested in the back of your head than the top of it. Focus your eyes on a spot on the wall behind the director's head. It will be less unnerving for both of you!
- Forewarn the director if you are dyslexic. He is bound to be sympathetic. Some very fine actors have this problem and your chances will not be prejudiced if you are open about it. Come prepared with a suitable audition piece so that the director can get a better idea of your work. He might agree to you doing that instead.
- Don't be fazed if the director asks you to give it another go but this time with a lisp. It shows he's interested and wants to see how versatile you are. Your previous rendition may even have given him a few ideas ...

Back in the early 1970s I auditioned for the part of the ill-favoured villain, De Flores, in Anthony Page's production of Middleton's The Changeling *for BBC TV. I knew I had read well. When I had finished there was a long pause and he said, 'That was very useful – now I know how it should be played.'*

T. P. McKenna (actor)

There is a seminal and witty little book on sight-reading by Nina Finburgh with illustrations by Anne McArthur (*Some Dos and Don't of Sight Reading for Actors at Audition*) published by Maverick Press, which I cannot recommend too highly. Smith and Kraus have published the American edition under the title *Hot Tips for Cold Readings*.

Sight-reading is a skill you *can* and *must* acquire. So many directors depend on it these days to make judgements about your suitability for a role. Practise for half an hour a day by reading aloud from a newspaper, a book of recipes, passages from a novel, your DIY manual – anything that will sharpen your skill and give you confidence. There is no doubt that in due course it will pay off.

The most wonderful thing in the world is to go to an interview expecting to read, expecting to go though hell and then to hear the director say, 'Well, as far as I'm concerned, the part is yours!'

Annette Badland (actor)

6 The Conventional Marketplace

This chapter offers specific information, tips and techniques for auditioning in individual areas of the conventional marketplace: theatre, musicals, television, film, commercials and voice-overs.

Theatre

Charles Marovitz was casting a new production of the Marovitz Hamlet, *which had been done three or four times before, and I was lucky enough to be asked to go along to meet him. I went along to his house in St John's Wood at ten o'clock as requested and rang the bell . . . No answer, so I banged on the door, then I rang the bell again, then I banged on the door until eventually the door opened and there is Marovitz in his dressing gown asking me to bring in the milk! I thought this was a bit off – I'd turned up at ten o'clock – in fact, I'd been up since about five thirty, worrying, and he's still in bed! I'd been given the brief to prepare two contrasting Shakespeare speeches. It turned out to be the most extraordinary audition I've ever had. The house was a three-storey town house so there were a number of landings on the staircase. After making me a cup of coffee Marovitz went up on to the first landing and told me to stay in the hallway. For my pieces I'd chosen 'Oh that this too, too solid flesh would melt' from* Hamlet *and a Chorus speech from* Henry V *before the battle, 'Now entertain conjecture of a time . . .' Two absolutely brilliant speeches . . . so I started off with* Hamlet *from the hallway. When I'd finished he told me to come up on to the first landing while he went up on to the second landing. He looked down at me and said, 'Now let's have the other one.' When I'd got to the end of that he instructed me to go up to the second landing while he came down to the first landing. I was totally confused by this time . . . 'Now,' he said slowly. 'let's have the words of the* Hamlet *speech with the emotional content of the* Henry V.' *I was quite excited by this and ready to have a go . . . Of course, it's what it's all about, isn't it . . . saying one thing but thinking something completely different? I got the job, I'm happy to say. Working with Marowitz was the only time in my whole career that I woke before my alarm and wished there were twenty-five hours in the day . . .*

David Schofield (actor)

Theatre auditions come in a variety of shapes and sizes, depending on whether they are for the Royal Shakespeare Company, a West End show, a provincial theatre or the fringe. They can take place almost anywhere, from cavernous auditoria to provincial living rooms with the director's cat prowling unnervingly around your chair. Both experiences will be equally familiar to the working actor.

Every director will have his own individual approach to casting. A director who knows your work might simply ask you to come in for a chat. You may be asked to read a few pages of the text that have been dispatched for you to work on, read from the text with the stage manager or improvise round a scene with other actors. More traditionally, audition pieces might be expected. Be prepared for absolutely anything!

Whenever a production is being cast, managements both great and small are always knee deep in submissions. For the two boys in Joe Orton's play *Loot* the West Yorkshire Playhouse saw forty actors. For *High Society* they saw 263 actors for fourteen parts. The West Yorkshire Playhouse mounts between fifteen and seventeen shows a year and will receive a thousand submissions or more for each production.

There are not many theatres left who can afford their own casting directors – the West Yorkshire Playhouse, the National, the RSC, the Manchester Royal Exchange, Scarborough and the Birmingham Rep being among the few – which makes the casting process in those theatres a little easier. Most are not so fortunate, so it is important submissions are carefully targeted. (You won't get a look-in with your English Rose credentials if they are casting a play by Wole Soyinka and by the time they are casting *Hay Fever* you will be lost under the avalanche!) Most theatre directors cast their own productions.

> *My role in the casting process is very dependent on the needs of each individual director. Most directors come with a list of names they want checking. I sit down with them, throw a few names around and we compile an 'ideal cast list'. You check it out and find that either they are all working or they can't or don't want to do it! After that most directors are willing to see actors who I think might be right even if they don't know them. Mainly they listen and see people I suggest. Most directors are open to suggestions because actors are what they survive on.*
> Kay Magson (Casting Director, West Yorkshire Playhouse)

Casting directors working for the larger companies wield considerable influence beyond their immediate sphere and are frequently approached by other theatre companies, TV, local film schools, etc. for casting advice. These casting directors can be found under individual theatres in *Contacts*.

Kay Magson files actors she knows under useful headings, so if, for instance, the Northern Film School want 'a Yorkshireman in his thirties, quite thickset' she is able to recommend a few likely candidates. She also organises annual auditions for local actors (anyone north of Birmingham prepared to travel) so if you qualify, these offer an opportunity of being seen by a major venue.

Few theatres hold general auditions in London. It's too expensive.

Regional theatres minimise wage bills by using local talent (they don't have to pay subsistence) so if you live in the regions, make yourself known to your local Rep, enquire about their talent-spotting procedures and keep tabs on forthcoming productions so you can target anything relevant.

Jude Kelly says that actors often mark letters to her 'Private and

Confidential'. If she is not in the building, they don't get opened at all – a point to be wary of.

Before making your submission, make sure you have the right experience for the job. Be realistic about what you can expect to be called up for. A couple of good parts on the fringe does not qualify you to play Hedda Gabler at Chichester, any more than passing your driving test does for racing at Brands Hatch. You won't get past first base, so save the postage. Target the plums on the fringe if your CV is thin. Consolidate your experience, build your repertoire and practise your craft before pitching for the National!

Directors can be tracked down and checked via *The Directory of Members* (The Director's Guild of Great Britain, Acorn House, 314–320 Grays Inn Road, London WC1X 8DB Tel: 020 7278 4343) which lists over one thousand Guild members with credits, contact addresses, telephone numbers and some indication of the area in which they work. Write to them at the theatre if they are doing a production. Remember that by the end of April a theatre may have a cast in the bag for a production in July. Reps often cast three productions ahead and could well be making casting decisions for shows even later in the season – so do allow yourself adequate lead time for submissions.

It's really difficult for actors who send unsolicited CVs and expect to get on to some sort of audition list, unless we happen to be casting a show at the time and the particular needs of the director seem to tie in with the submission. The director's job is to study the play and arrive at a strong sense of what the character is – what the content of the play suggests in terms of character type. They are bound to either want to work with people they've enjoyed working with before or with people they've seen in performances they admire on film, television or radio . . . You can't escape from the fact that the more high-profile a theatre is, the more demand there is on the actor to (a) have quite a lot of experience in certain roles and (b) have a certain amount of flair, charisma or competence. So although we give out more jobs, there might be a narrowing effect in some respects because we will be looking at people who have an acknowledged level of competence in the industry. Of course, you are looking for talented newcomers as well, but they will mainly be sought for those smaller parts . . . That must feel awfully exclusive to people trying to get in . . . But both Kay [Magson] *and I have the philosophy, 'Being heard of is not the criterion – being good is the criterion!' Being helped to be 'more good' by being here* [the West Yorkshire Playhouse] *is also very important to us.*

Jude Kelly (Artistic Director, West Yorkshire Playhouse)

Musicals

With the growing popularity of musicals, an actor who can sing stands a much better chance of working than the actor who can't. If you can make a song 'live' and communicate its message, you will have a strong advantage over a singer who can do little more than hit all the notes in the middle. You don't have to sound like Kiri Te Kanawa or Pavarotti: Judi Dench and Michael Crawford are but two actors who have a way with a song that is entirely satisfying. Even if you don't think of yourself as a 'singer' it is certainly worth your while to learn how to perform a song. It's an important skill to have in your armoury.

Find a singing teacher

There are a comparatively small number of singing teachers around who specialise in coaching for the musical theatre. Some are rather expensive, so shop around. You should expect to pay at least £30 per hour. Unlike opera, where a singer will usually only be required to perform two or three times a week, in a musical you may have up to eight performances a week to cope with. Consequently your voice needs to develop considerable stamina, so a teacher who understands about show music – and increasingly how to use a body mike – is an absolute must. A singing teacher who plays the piano and works from home is likely to be less expensive than a teacher who has to hire an accompanist and a studio. You should ask your teacher to supply you with tailor-made exercises to suit your voice and a taped accompaniment of your songs pitched for your voice so that you can practise at home if you are unable to get to lessons. A teacher who understands the genre will not only help you to find and develop your singing voice and assist with any technical or physical problems you might encounter, he will also advise you about presentation and interpretation, tackling everything from issues of confidence and focus to pointers on how to end a song and acknowledge applause.

The Incorporated Society of Musicians (020 7629 4413), the professional association for teachers and performers, publishes a register of music teachers. There is a section on singing teachers, which gives details of each teacher's location and particular areas of expertise. It is called the *ISM Register of Professional and Private Music Teachers* and costs £16 but is also available free in the reference section of the website (www.ism.org) or in main public libraries. It lists teachers of musical instruments as well.

Alternatively, the Association of Teachers of Singing (AOTOS, Weir House, 108 Newton Road, Burton-upon-Trent, Staffs DE15 OTT Tel: 01283 542198) publishes a directory of around 500 singing teachers across the country.

Choosing a song

Very useful for repertoire is *The Singer's Music Theatre Anthology*, which comes in nine volumes and contains a rich selection of show songs from the last fifty years. There are volumes for sopranos, mezzos and contraltos, baritones, basses, 'belter numbers' and duets. The anthologies are published in the USA by the Leonard Publishing Corporation and are obtainable at Chappell's in New Bond Street, London, who incidentally have the largest single selection of show music in the world. They stock the album for almost any musical of the last thirty years, and many general anthologies of songs by composers like Gershwin and Sondheim. Your singing teacher will help you choose a variety of songs to suit your voice and personality.

Musical auditions
Some dos and don'ts . . .

- Be prepared. Singing auditions are often thrust upon you at short notice. Make sure you work on your numbers regularly between singing lessons and keep them in good shape. Check with your music teacher whether your accompaniment on tape will cost you any extra. Sing in the shower. Do your exercises while you are ironing. The wonderful thing about singing is that you can practise it almost anywhere, although the cheese counter at Sainsbury's might raise the odd eyebrow!
- Be flexible. You may have planned to move downstage right at a certain point in your song but when you get to the audition you find yourself trapped by lighting cables or blocked by a baby grand. Make sure you rehearse your songs in a variety of ways so that you are not thrown by unfamiliar geography.
- Be original! Some numbers are worked to death and yet another rendition of 'Memory', 'Summertime' or 'I Feel Pretty' (particularly if you're not) will cause any audition panel to blench. Unless, of course, you sing the definitive version!

We were casting a production of Betjemania *which I had devised with John Gould and which was to run at the King's Head in Islington. We wanted two girls and two boys – they all had been told they had to sing, so they each came prepared with a song or two. This was first thing in the morning. I can't even remember the girl's name. She said she was going to sing 'I Feel Pretty'. It was a freezing-cold rehearsal room. We had a coal fire but it was never working at ten in the morning. She was wearing leggings and goodness knows what else to try to keep warm. When she'd finished I said, 'Why did you choose to sing that song?' Defiantly she said, 'Because I do!' with her little nose all blue.*

David Benedictus (actor and novelist)

- Sing something you are comfortable with and have lived with for a long time. It's better to sing a song that's rooted and confident, even if it doesn't suit the style of the show you are auditioning for, than to throw something more appropriate together in a couple of afternoons and expect your singing teacher to perform a miracle. It is a mistake to think that singing a suitable song badly will stand you in better stead than singing an unsuitable one well.

- Build a repertoire. The more songs you have under your belt, the better. A varied selection might include a ballad, a 'point' number, a comic song, something 'up-tempo', a bit of jazz, a folk song, something risqué, a song from a musical. Above all, make sure you have a couple of songs that show off your personality and the full range and versatility of your voice.

- Wear clothes that make you feel comfortable and happy. It is your singing voice, your confidence and your CV that will get you the job. There is no need to dress for the part.

- Discard your outdoor clothing in a dressing room or green room before you go in. There is nothing more demoralising than fumbling with buttons, bags, scarves and scores when you are feeling nervous. If you have to take your coat into the audition room drop it discreetly at the side of the stage or by the door. Make sure you remember to collect it on the way out. An apologetic head round the door five minutes later won't do much for your grand exit!

- Make sure your music is marked at the right place so you don't have to fumble to find your song and then *hand it to the accompanist before doing anything else.* That way he will have time to acquaint himself with the music while you are chatting to the director.

- Make sure you have a clearly marked copy of the score. The accompanist is not a thought reader! You may have decided to cut the introduction and repeat the chorus, and your accompanist will need clear instructions to that effect. Scribbled directions on the page, perhaps from a previous performance, will confuse and mislead. Actors are generally rushed through musical auditions at a humiliating rate, so you may not have time to take the accompanist through your score.

- Don't ever assume that an accompanist can transpose your song on sight. If he has this skill, be quite clear which key you want: 'I'd like it higher, please' won't do! A Cole Porter or Richard Rodgers number will have a clear piano line but more contemporary songs are often conceived for orchestral accompaniment and are much more difficult to play. You must see it as your responsibility to provide a score in the right key for your voice. It might cost a few pounds to commission an arranger but it will certainly be in your best interest.

- Before launching into your audition, take time to sing a few bars to your accompanist to demonstrate the tempo of your song. If the tempo changes halfway through, show him clearly where and how it happens. If he fails to follow your instructions, don't adapt your speed to his. Stick to your guns and hope that the pianist will be sensitive enough to adapt. Most self-respecting musical directors will know where the fault, if any, lies.

- If you have your own accompanist (there will be no objection to taking him along if you want to) make sure he really can cut the mustard. An accompanist is an expensive luxury and you will look just as professional if you manage to cope successfully with the accompanist provided at the audition.

- Be seen to check the lights if your audition is in a theatre. It looks as if you know what you are doing. You may find you are required to sing in a centre-stage pool. Make sure you stand firmly in the centre, and don't loiter on the edge, so you are lit to best advantage.

- Keep your song short. Some show songs are interminable and, given the constraints of the audition process, you are bound to be cut off in your prime. You will never know whether they were running against the clock or just thought you were awful! Better a polished flash of brilliance . . .

- Announce your number simply and without elaboration. The full story of *Company* will not be appreciated.

- Avoid physical tics and clichés – pumping gestures with your arms, for instance, or 'holding trays', as teacher Betty Roe describes a typical singing pose. Better to clasp your hands gently in front of you than articulate your song with gestures that are not spontaneous.

- Approach your song in exactly the same way as you would a piece of text (see chapter 5). Your performance should indicate that you can act as well as sing.
- Trust the good work you have done at home and with your teacher. Many auditions take place in the 'dry acoustic' of a dance studio or church hall. Don't force your voice because it sounds different from the way it sounds in your lesson or a practice situation. Even the most experienced singers find a 'dry acoustic' hard to come to terms with.
- Remember to collect your music and thank the pianist when you have finished. The accompanist at musical auditions is often the musical director. He deserves to be thanked anyway.

An open audition can be demoralising and humiliating. It's quite common for actors to be lined up and each asked to sing ten bars of a song while casting personnel talk, shuffle papers and drink cups of tea. You are unlikely to get a job this way, unless you have exceptional talent, but if you can acquit yourself well at an 'open', you will develop the thick skin and confidence necessary for absolutely anything that follows!

At a recall audition, you may be asked to 'move'. This means dance! There is usually some form of dancing in a show that involves everyone and they need to make sure you don't have two left feet and no co-ordination. If you're not the best dancer in the world, go at it with gusto, don't look too worried and keep smiling. That way you won't be too occupied about what your feet are doing!

Deborah McHardy (actor/singer)

And remember, 'Thank you very much' does not necessarily mean 'Goodbye for ever'!

I was doing panto in Coventry and had made the trip to London for a morning audition with the assistant director of the Bristol Old Vic. I gave him my Juliet. He seemed very pleased and asked me if I could come back in the afternoon to meet the director. I readily agreed and spent the three-hour wait fantasising about playing a line of juve leads in Bristol. (This was in the days when such a thing as a 'line of parts' existed!) When the time came for my recall, I stepped out on to the stage, as before, and looked confidently into the dark. I launched into my piece . . .

> *Gallop apace you fiery footed steeds*
> *Towards Phoebus' lodging. Such a waggoner*
> *As . . .*

'Thank you,' the director's voice stopped me. I thought I must have misheard. 'Thank you very much,' he said again. My jaw dropped open. 'Is that it?' I said rather lamely. 'Thank you very much,' came the final dismissal. I was gobsmacked. I'd come all this way, had hung around for three hours . . . and been asked to come back here. For this? I was really upset. The unbelievable impersonality of the rejection was truly shocking. And yet I felt so disadvantaged by the whole situation that I couldn't find one word to protest at my ill treatment. I shook with rage and the injustice of it, all the way back to Coventry.

Elizabeth Mansfield (actor/singer)

A lot of a director's time is spent in thinking of ways to say 'no' to actors nicely, without destroying such confidence as they may have. When I was working in BBC Television, I was casting the Arch-Vicar in Aldous Huxley's Ape and Essence. *The Arch-Vicar is a strange eccentric part – and apart from anything else he is a eunuch. I had in mind an old actor called Ernest Milton, who was, in his day, extremely famous, very eccentric and liked a glass or two, so they told me. He was in his early nineties and I thought it would be absolutely brilliant if we could have Ernest Milton. However, it was very difficult to know, without meeting him, whether he would be up to it. So I invited him along to Television Centre, but I knew as soon as he came through the door that I had made a mistake. He was too decrepit. On the other hand, this grand old man of English Theatre clearly thought that an invitation to Television Centre was tanta-*

mount to an offer. He also clearly needed the money. It was extremely difficult and I tried to find ways of getting off the hook. I tried, 'Well, it isn't actually a very large part you know . . .' 'Nice little cameo,' he responded enthusiastically. I tried every tack until finally, in desperation, I ventured, 'You do realise, Mr Milton, that the Arch-Vicar is a eunuch.' There was a long pause. 'No,' he said very grandly, 'I don't think my public would go for that!'

David Benedictus (actor, novelist)

Television

Television programme providers range from the Independent Television Network and BBC channels to cable and satellite TV, with Channel 5 and digital terrestrial broadcasting. Output is phenomenal, providing bread-and-butter work for actors in soap operas, plays, sitcoms, series and British TV films. Many an actor has paid his bills with TV residuals in a bad year.

It is hard for actors to find work in television without an agent, but not impossible. Look out for breakdowns in the casting information sheets (see chapter 4) or the Actors Centre noticeboard (see page 79). TV directors tend to cast actors whose work they know or through submissions from a trusted coterie of agents to whom they will probably have given detailed character breakdowns.

It's a question of trust between the director and the agent . . . Some considerable time ago I was casting a play with a very tall actress and we'd been let down by an actor at the last minute. Suddenly I had this brainwave. A brilliant actor. I won't name him. So I offered him the part there and then. Pretty soon his agent was on the line to me saying, 'You do know how tall your actress is, don't you? My client is only four foot eleven!' And of course he was absolutely right. They were both magnificent actors but they wouldn't have matched. Thank God he reminded me. He would have had to stand on a ladder!

Leonard Lewis (television producer)

It's an expensive chore sending your CV and photograph to every TV producer, director and casting director in *Contacts*, but it's probably worth it. Casting directors are particularly important individuals in television. A director will work closely with them, discussing the script and its casting requirements in great detail. It is often on a casting director's say-so that actors are invited to audition. TV casting directors will often ask to see your showreel.

When you arrive for your audition, make yourself known to the receptionist and say whom you've come to see, but don't expect your audition to be on time. Auditionees are late, don't turn up at all or they take twice as long as expected, so you may have to hang around for some time.

You generally won't have seen the script beforehand, unless you are auditioning for a major part. Arrive early and ask if a script can be sent down. If your agent hasn't already made it clear, try to ascertain more about the character you are up for. Skim through the script to see if you can get the general drift, then focus on those scenes that feature your character. Try to glean as much as you can from the text. More often than not you will only be given a couple of relevant pages, so you won't be able to get much of a handle on the character from those – but you *can* still play the situation. You are *hurt and angry* because your boyfriend has cheated on you … You are *drunk and defiant* as a policeman stops your car … You are *perplexed and worried* because your child has not come home from school …

When you are called, listen carefully to instructions about where to go. If the production secretary doesn't meet you at the lift, wandering round the corridors will be unsettling. You may have another wait in a corridor or nearby empty office with several other contenders before you are finally called in to meet the director. Bear in mind they may not all be auditioning for the same part!

Television interviews often take place in a space especially set aside for the purpose, but you can find yourself battling with the paraphernalia of past and future productions, interruptions and ringing telephones. Try not to be distracted. The conveyor belt of television production must go on!

The director is unlikely to meet you on his own, so listen carefully to introductions to other production personnel, then you can address them by name. These will be key people in the forthcoming production and will be consulted about your suitability after you have gone. The casting director will almost certainly be there, so you will have an ally.

The interview will rarely be longer than twenty minutes and usually consists of a brief warm-up chat, followed by a 'cold-reading' for which you will now be well prepared (see chapter 5).

If you feel you will do better to stand rather than sit to articulate the scene, remember that the director will be observing the thought process in your face and eyes, and the emotion in your voice – not how well you can mime a perfect passage through swing doors. Keep it focused. Keep it simple. Choose an approach to the text that allows the director to watch your face. If you think and feel the right things, they will be communicated to your audience.

The director may be so impressed with your audition that he makes a mental note to ring your agent the moment you leave the office. You can be ninety-nine per cent certain that he won't tell you! Instead of that instant unequivocal offer, you will hear . . . 'We've got several more people to see . . .' or 'We'll let you know . . .' The director won't want to commit himself before confirming his decision with other relevant production personnel and talking to your agent about dates and money. And who knows what spangled genius might be waiting in the corridor?

There is an apocryphal story about the famous director who clasped an actor's hand at the end of his audition, looked deep into his eyes and said, 'I'm going to make you a star!' The actor walked out of the office on cloud nine and never heard another word!

If the director is interested but unsure, he may ask you to read the scene again in another way – or to read a completely different one. For a really important part you may be called back so that the team can make a final decision. Television production is highly pressurised, so recalls are rarely gratuitous. At this point you or your agent are perfectly within your rights to ask why a recall is necessary and how many others are being considered. A recall either means that you are (a) a hot contender but the director can't make up his mind, or (b) that the director has made up his mind but there are others to be persuaded or required to confirm his choice, or (c) he needs to confirm how well you match up with other characters – especially if the audition is for a series. Whatever the reason, a recall is usually a good sign and you should attend feeling confident in the work you did at your first audition. If the choice goes against you in the end, you will have made your mark and should nurture your contact with that director.

Should I work as an extra?

If you have no TV credits on your CV, working as an extra (non-speaking crowd artist) will give you a unique opportunity to watch how television production works, either in the studio or on location, and be paid for the privilege. A limited amount of extra work did nobody's career any harm. (David Niven was spotted in the crowd!) It provides another opportunity to network and earns you around £60 per day. This increases pro rata if you make an individual appearance or are given a word or two to say. You can learn a great deal from listening and watching. I have seen no evidence that it prevents good actors being offered proper roles.

There is a list of extras and walk-ons agents in *Contacts*.

Film

> *If you are auditioning for a movie – unless it's an action movie – you must remember it all happens in the eyes – in what the actor's thinking. So if you are auditioning for somebody on video camera and the camera never sees your eyes because you're looking at the script, then they're not going to see any performance – so if I can, I always learn it. It's not trying to be teacher's pet. It's purely for practical reasons . . .*

> David Schofield (actor)

A major film generally has worldwide distribution, enhancing an actor's reputation and profile, and providing a valuable showcase for his talent. Not surprisingly, a good performance in a well-distributed film ups your ante considerably!

An audition for a film is not called an 'audition' but a 'meeting', which will usually be with the director and possibly the producer and casting director as well. It can take place anywhere from the director's hotel (if it is an American or foreign film) to the film company's local offices. There might be a video camera at this first meeting, but it is unlikely. Take your showreel along. You can expect a relaxed and encouraging affair where every attempt is made to make you feel at ease.

You will almost certainly be sent the script, or the relevant pages, beforehand, so you should have time to do some worthwhile preparation. If your agent can possibly get hold of the whole script, so much the better. That way you can trace your character, how he interacts with other characters and the role he plays in the development of the storyline. Even if you haven't been sent the whole script, make sure your agent can fill you in on the storyline and character. Work as hard as you possibly can on the text, learn your lines inside out, back to front – concentrating not only on what your character is thinking and feeling while he is *speaking*, but while he is *listening* too.

In an interview with Anthony Hopkins, Barry Norman once asked if it was true that he read the script a hundred times. 'No,' replied Mr Hopkins. 'Absolutely not. I read it two hundred times!' Take a leaf out of his book. By the time you arrive at your test, you must be so comfortable with the scenes you are to play that even the most bizarre piece of direction won't throw your concentration off balance.

Films are shot in moments and a reaction can often be more important than a line of dialogue. Simon Callow describes film acting as 'admitting the camera into your aura ... a little like being X-rayed'. The camera can spot the sweat on a thought, so play the situation as truthfully and with as much commitment as you can. You may be asked to read with a casting director of little acting talent, or an old pro especially imported for the job. Don't be deflected from the detailed conscientious work you did at home. If you 'don't get your ball back' from the other actor, react as if you had. Take control. It's *you* the director will be focusing on!

I was working on one of the Sherlock Holmes films with a wonderful director called Peter Hammond, and an actress on the film was having problems with a scene. It was a close-up and she had to turn to camera to reveal a bad facial scar. Peter Hammond handled it brilliantly. I will always remember what he said . . . 'Just regard the frame of the camera as the proscenium arch. In a big close-up you are the set, the emotion, the lights – everything.' And of course he was absolutely right.

Edward Hardwicke (actor)

They came over to shoot two episodes of Remington Steel *here with Pierce Brosnan and Stephanie Zimbalist. I went up for this part – went to this hotel somewhere in the West End – and I was shown into this big panelled conference room. There must have been twelve people sitting down the long side of this table, and I was asked to sit on the other side of it, opposite them. I began the long walk from the door, had reached the chair and was just about to sit down when one of them said, 'Thank you. Thank you very much. Thank you.' My bum didn't even touch the seat and I was out again! I slunk away feeling like the most miserable failure. I thought, 'God, they didn't even give me a chance . . .' That afternoon my agent phoned and said, 'OK David! You got it.' I was obviously exactly what they were looking for.*

David Quilter (actor)

If it is not a major part, you can be offered the job quite quickly on the basis of a first sighting. If you are being seen for a more important role, you might be invited back for a screen test. Your test will almost certainly be shot on video, because it's cheaper and more flexible than film. At this stage you will probably be on a shortlist of three or four. A test can take place anywhere from a hotel to the casting director's office with anything from a single video camera operator to a more lavish set-up in a studio – depending on the size and budget of the film. You could be asked to test two or three times while the director mulls over his options. Try to stay calm. Don't let the camera spot your anxiety. If you have got this far, it won't be your talent that's in question – more likely the decision will hang on something unalterable, like your colouring. Tests may occur over weeks or even months. Films can be delayed or shelved as backers get cold feet or locations fall through. No snow. An unexpected monsoon. That long-forgotten test you did just before Christmas can deliver a job ten months later. Film-making is a lengthy, frustrating and complex business.

If you get a part in a movie you will probably be booked for a guaranteed number of days over so many weeks. You will be paid for those days whether you work them or not, and if you work more days you will be paid extra. Your agent will negotiate your fee plus a daily rate for the job – £700 a day would not be unusual, although increasingly there seems to be a 'take-it-or-leave-it' offer on the table for smaller parts.

Commercials

> I was called in for one commercial where they wanted a 'New Age spiritualist'. But they didn't want a hippy! 'Someone sort of "beat",' they said, 'and if you can chant, it would be good.' Well, I don't have long hair. I don't have pierced ears. I don't have tattoos. When I think of a New Age traveller I think of a sort of pseudo-half-grunge punk, a traveller in a tent, going to rock festivals. You're into 'Let's interpret what we think they might want . . .' It turned out what they were looking for was a nutty California guru flake. The ad was selling some kind of peanuts! Some pun about nuts and California I think . . . ?
>
> Robert Jezek (actor)

Almost every actor wants to do commercials! A regular TV advertisement for a leading product can set you up nicely with fees and residuals, so you can accept interesting but low-paid work without having to worry.

You are unlikely to get commercial castings without an agent (there are agents who deal with commercial castings only). But it is your photograph that is your ticket through the door of a commercial casting – you will be called in to the casting purely on the basis of it. The client will generally be looking for 'types' – glamorous grandmas, friendly dads, young mums with whiter than white washing, teenagers who need spot cream. You will not be popular if you have chopped your waist-length hair or shaved your head since the photograph was taken. For commercials you should certainly suggest your suitability for the job by what you wear for the casting, so you need to give some thought to your wardrobe. If you are a tall, middle-aged man with short hair and clean-cut features, it would be counter-productive not to own at least one good business suit. A modest selection of props will be useful too. Spectacle frames, an earring, a cravat – anything that might make you more distinctive.

Press your agent to glean maximum information about the ad. Briefs can be horribly sketchy. One casting director listed some amusing client requests:

An American businessman who is exhausted.
A Prince and a Vampire.
Forest Gump when running!?
A bon viveur on his thirty-fifth birthday.
A man who drives a caravan and can tap-dance.
Mafioso, late thirties.
Zany presenter.
Man who speaks Japanese.
Wild rock singer.
A man who looks as if he comes out of his skin . . . ?

Going for a commercial can be a deeply humiliating experience. You go into some god-awful little room in Soho to meet these people, who don't usually give you the time of day. The only person who might possibly be on your wavelength is the director. You can get some very big movie directors directing commercials. I always make a point when I go for a commercial interview of going round everybody and shaking their hand because they are not necessarily going to as much as look up at you and you want them to remember. As far as they are concerned the actor is just part of the commodity and they can be extremely rude.

David Quilter (actor)

The commercial interview is pure business. The powerful wild card in the pack is the client. He may be the company's managing director or marketing director – some big cheese in the company. He is the one you have to please. The director may think you are the next Jude Law but if the client doesn't see you as the face of Product X, his view will undoubtedly prevail. Don't take it personally. It has less than nothing to do with your skill as an actor.

Often the first thing you are asked to do on arrival is identify yourself on camera. (Your 'ident'.) You may be auditioning for the client, the director and the casting director or you may find yourself auditioning for no more than the casting director and camera operator. In this case the video of your audition will be dispatched to the director and client for their perusal in due course.

Look directly into the lens and give your name clearly, the name of your agent and your height. You could be asked if you have done any other ads for the same country. This is important. They sometimes won't want you if you are already identified with another product. Hopefully your agent has done his homework. If you have been used in a prominent advertising campaign, make sure your agent has negotiated fees that reflect time 'out of circulation' when you can't do other ads, although sometimes this is difficult to judge without the benefit of hindsight. Nobody could have guessed how successful the Yellow Pages 'messy flat' ad would become!

After your 'ident' you will be told something about the concept, the script and the product. The chat might take place 'on camera' as part of your audition. It doesn't matter if you talk about your last TV appearance or your new baby. Give the camera an opportunity to look into your eyes and see your face from a number of angles. Ring the changes. Be warm. Be engaging. Be serious. It's not *Hamlet*. Relax. Write yourself a little script and rehearse it at home. The client and director want to feel the 'texture' of your personality.

The client's 'concept' may be hazy. The director may or may not be there. Listen carefully to what everyone has to say. Remember, the client is not a 'man of the theatre' but a businessman, usually with little or no understanding of the language actors use to communicate about a play's subtext – about relationships, character and interpretation. Most of the time you will have very little script on which to base a performance, so probe sensitively. Does he envisage a particular style? Naturalism? Larger than life? Hard sell? How does he see the character? It sometimes helps to use well-known personalities as benchmarks. 'Is he a Woody Allen type?' 'Perhaps a touch of the Marilyn Monroes . . . ?' 'Would you like it performed to you or to camera?' Help him clarify his vision. Often he won't have much of one and unless your agent has been able to get some idea of his requirements, you are in the business of trying to second-guess what he wants. What helps you helps him. The casting director may be as perplexed as you are, so you could find a rich variety of 'New Age gurus' or 'exhausted American businessmen' waiting to be seen. Don't be fazed. They are just as likely to choose you as one of the others. And it's not unknown for a script to be altered to accommodate an actor's wacky and original interpretation. Nothing in the world of advertising is written in stone.

If you are asked to read a short piece of script or improvise a scene, this is also likely to take place 'on camera'. This is your moment. Take a beat. Don't rush. Turn upstage from the camera to give yourself time to ingest any messages you may have been given about the product and the scene. Be bold. Make a sure-footed choice that will show your range and versatility. You may be working with another actor who is a complete stranger. If this is the case, give the other performer his space. You won't do yourself any favours if you are seen to be greedy or selfish on camera. On the other hand, be firm if he does not respect yours. Make your interpretation of the scene varied and imaginative. If you give the client the opportunity to say 'I liked that bit when . . .', you will have something to work with and develop from. You will know he is interested! Be courteous to the camera operator. He can give you that sensitive close-up or focus on your left ear.

Being 'pencilled'

If the client likes you at your casting, doesn't want to lose you but has seen a couple of other actors he likes as well, he will put 'a pencil' on you, which means that the casting director has first call on your services on that particular day. It is not a booking! 'A pencil' or 'a heavy pencil' means, 'We're ninety-nine per cent certain we're going to use you, but...' Your agent is bound (by some mystic and unwritten code of honour) to abide by that 'pencil' even if Ken Loach wants you on the same day. Some clients are so insecure they 'pencil' half the actors they see, just to be on the safe side – so don't get too excited. If they can't make up their minds, you may be recalled. Your agent should ask why you are being recalled, how many other actors are being recalled and what you will have to do – then you will have a realistic idea of your chances. When you are offered the job six months later, try to remember what you did and what you wore on the day (keep a note in your filing system about that yellow cardigan or gran's pince nez)! If they want you to wear your own clothes in the ad they may get their own modest fee!

Equity has had a negotiated agreement in place since 1991 for television commercials, which most reputable advertisers still honour, and which covers, among other things, the basic studio fee and a system of use fees (repeats). The basic studio fee is negotiable and your agent will obviously try to get the best deal he can for you. A sum in the region of £200–£300 is a common daily shooting fee, although the wallet buckles at what big names can command for promoting leading products! This fee covers the actual work you do on the day of the shoot and may be enhanced through overtime and the like.

Use fees are only payable to the Featured Artist – defined by the TV Commercials Agreement as 'someone whose individual role plays an essential part in the telling of the commercial story'. They are calculated on a complex formula, which takes account of both your original daily fee and the viewing figures. Commercials shown at peak viewing times will achieve higher earnings than those shown only after the late-night horror movie.

If you make a commercial in this country which is subsequently used overseas, then Equity has a scale of payment for this use which is based on a multiple of your original daily fee. This is often referred to as a 'buyout'. The multiple will take account of the overseas market. For example, a 400 per cent 'buyout' will be four times your daily fee for a year.

If a commercial is being made outside the UK then the Equity agreement is not binding and you will probably be offered a buyout based on your original fee to cover one or more years' use of the commercial. Most agents have their own detailed contract for this purpose.

Payments are also due for what are known as 'ancillary' uses of the commercial – i.e. any other use than it being transmitted on television. These are many and varied, and negotiating payments can be tricky. Let your agent wrestle the Leviathan! That's what you pay him for.

It was some time in the late 1970s . . . I can't remember which show . . . a young actress came to audition for me, we were chatting at the end of it and I said, 'So, what are you doing at the moment?' She said, 'I'm off to Amsterdam this weekend. I'm filming a recruitment commercial for the Dutch Army. I have to dance on a table in bra and panties. They put these small electric charges in the cups of the bra and they blow off.' 'Good God,' I said. 'Is this dangerous?' She said, 'Do you think it might be . . . ?'

Graham Devlin (director)

I was up for an ad for some headache pills, Phensic, I think it was. 'Make like you've got a headache,' instructed the American director. I pulled what I thought was an appropriate headache face. 'No dear,' he said patronisingly, 'I said a headache, not a fractured skull.'

Patricia Maynard (actor)

Radio Drama

Because the radio audience has only its ears and not its eyes, it has to work harder than an audience sharing the experience of a visual and auditory performance. It has to decode the information it hears and use its imagination.

The actors on radio have to work harder too. In an anonymous room called a studio, working in an unrealistic spatial relationship to each other against a microphone which represents the ears and the mind of the audience of one (radio listening is usually a unique experience), the actor's imagination has to create the true spatial relationship with other characters in a scene: the way they are all dressed/costumed, the environment they inhabit (i.e. the set), the furniture they use, the props they handle – the bicycle pump with a cork popping is a bottle of Bollinger, the studio water poured from a jug into a glass of Andrew's Liver Salts is the effervescent champagne itself. 'Mmmm [sip], lovely!'

The actors must create the distance of the balcony scene by the right amount of pitch in the voice, the feeling of heavy seas and high winds by a different kind of vocalisation against the (unheard by them) forces of nature, the fury and exhaustion of battle against the clattering of well-used studio swords which they themselves might – just might – be allowed to wield. It's all the Emperor's clothes: a wonderful world of lies and simulation; the apotheosis of the absurd.

John Tydeman (former head of BBC Radio Drama)

There is obviously no such thing as a 'radio actor' – a good actor is good in any medium – but there *are* actors whom the microphone adores, actors with distinctive voices, who are truthful on mike and fire our imaginations with the power of theirs. They are often required to play more than one role convincingly.

I remember once I had to read a short story from Sri Lanka. There were about twenty-six characters in it, from children to servants, to old and young men and women, and even a group of monks chanting the Buddhist refrain. 'Buddham, sharanam, gacchaamee . . .' When it was broadcast, a friend from the Hindi section at Bush House had obviously not taken in the announcement: 'BBC World Service Short Story. This week's story is from Sri Lanka, the reader Saeed Jaffrey', because he came up to me and said. 'Saeed, who else was in that play with you?' Made my day. Made my month.

Saeed Jaffrey (actor)

Most plays are recorded in the studio but an increasing number are recorded on location. Ibsen's *Doll's House*, for instance, was recorded by Cherry Cookson – one of the pioneers of location broadcasting – in a house in Highgate!

Radio producers seem very prepared to do their homework in a quest for new and interesting voices, casting from TV, theatre and, increasingly, film. They seek strong, confident and versatile performers who can make the necessary rapid commitment to a performance.

> *The essence of modern radio is speed. With ever-decreasing budgets and less time in the studio, the onus is on the actor to deliver the goods quickly and efficiently with the minimum of fuss. You are expected to have done your homework thoroughly, researched into accents, dialects, etc. so that when you arrive in the studio you are on the edge of being ready to record. Sadly there is less and less time for discussion and experiment. I was once phoned at 10 p.m. to go into the studios at 9.30 a.m. to play Ian Smith [former Rhodesian PM] in a reconstruction of a 1960s telephone conversation he had with Harold Wilson, for a news programme – not long to sharpen up the South African accent!*
>
> David Timson (actor)

As an example of the pace of working, it is quite possible to arrive in the studio at 10 a.m., meet the actors in your scene, often for the first time, and have the definitive recording 'laid down' by 10.30 a.m.

The BBC's commitment to new talent is confirmed by the Carleton Hobbs BBC Radio Drama Bursary Award, which has been going since 1953. Around ninety competitors from accredited drama schools across the country enter every year. The 'prize' is a coveted six-month contract with the Radio Drama Company (RDC) – afffectionately known as the Radio Rep. This is a body of around ten or twelve versatile actors with a broad range of vocal ages and accents between them. Previous winners include Freddie Jones, David Threlfall, Samantha Bond and Emma Fielding.

> *Every day on the Rep was different. Every script I was given threw up a new challenge for me, be it an accent, age or difficult scene. The plays I took part in ranged from those of Shakespeare, an adaptation of an Emile Zola novel, an episode of* Inspector Morse, *a musical and a five-part Agatha Christie. Then, of course, there were all the readings on* Woman's Hour, Kaleidoscope *and not forgetting the wonderful world of light entertainment . . .*
>
> Tracy Wiles (Carleton Hobbs winner 1995)

In addition to the Carleton Hobbs, the BBC tracks down fresh talent and recruits for the RDC through a system of workshops (eight actors per workshop, which are run approximately five or six times a year.). Each workshop aims to target a particular age group. They try to create a 'real-life' situation in which actors can relax and show off their range, intelligence and ability to work with others. The Corporation is particularly keen to attract more black and Asian actors on to the RDC and to their work in general.

How can you be selected for a workshop?

> *When we ran the old general auditions there were always a couple of actors who would take you on a round-Britain tour with pieces they had written themselves, which was designed to demonstrate their versatility. Every accent in the book from Scunthorpe to Scots! Just as you were getting your ear tuned to one accent, they were on to the next. Very difficult to listen to. I wouldn't advise actors to do that. We are looking for genuine accents, not 'my best attempt at . . .'*
>
> Janet Whitaker (senior radio producer)

To participate in a workshop, you need to be nominated by a producer who in turn will recommend you to a committee of producers (the RDC Committee) who will want to see your work.

As soon as you have a play, rehearsed reading, TV or film to draw to the Committee's attention, identify a handful of producers whose work you know and write to them. Radio drama producers never cast from demo-tapes, so don't waste your money by sending these as well. Offer them free seats to your show if you are working. Send reviews. If you have any small lever, any modest contact – use it. A recommendation from an established broadcaster might effect an introduction. Nobody will stick his or her neck out without confidence in your ability, so a producer might listen to that.

Whatever else you do, *listen to the radio!* It is impertinent not to if you are looking for work on the airwaves. You will learn an awful lot about radio acting technique from listening with an educated ear; and if you happen to hear a producer's production, you can refer to it warmly in any correspondence.

Once admitted to a workshop you will audition alongside seven other performers on a variety of two-handed scenes (classic, modern, comic, etc.). Four producers will direct you over the course of a morning or afternoon – giving you a crash course in the art and technique of working at the microphone. This gives them a chance to explore your skills, strengths and weaknesses. You will be asked to sight-read a straight piece of fiction to aid castings for readings and short stories, and perform a piece of your own choosing, which gives you an opportunity to impress with your 'high kicks, tightrope-walking and splits'!

Many newcomers are employed on radio through the workshop process but a few producers do have a policy of scouting out talent on their own account and cast actors new to the medium in smaller parts without any formal audition. It's a low-risk strategy that sometimes allows good performers in through the back door. Some have been known to invite actors in to the office to read, but with increasing pressure on time and money, this public service is becoming rarer.

The good news is that actors invited to attend the workshops stand a very good chance of being offered freelance engagements within radio. If you are chosen for the RDC you will be offered a three-month contract – renewable for a further three months if appropriate. You can look forward to a short period of secure and challenging employment.

Bonuses of working in radio

Most actors are keen to do radio because, apart from being a challenging medium, it gives them the chance to play roles they might never play elsewhere. Annette Badland in her early forties played the young Anne Gedge in David Halliwell's *Little Malcolm and His Struggle against the Eunuchs* and was 'the best Anne Gedge' the playwright had ever 'seen'!

The short timescale of productions (three days for a ninety-minute play) means that radio work can be slipped in quite easily between other jobs. And there are no lines to learn!

The medium also provides unique opportunities to work with eminent actors. As a youngster I had the honour of playing scenes with Dame Sybil Thorndike. Nowadays you might work with film stars like Kathleen Turner and television stars like Sharon Gless.

Over a third of radio's output is produced outside London, at regional centres of production in Manchester, Edinburgh, Belfast, Cardiff and Birmingham, so opportunities for actors living in the regions is good. A number of the regions have their own local audition procedures. Local actors should make enquiries.

If you have no broadcasting experience but feel you might have a flair for it, the Actors Centre runs some excellent classes with skilled broadcasters. The City Lit runs a course too (see chapter 9).

The first radio play I ever did was a play called The Chalk Garden *which Edith Evans had starred in on the stage many years earlier and now, as a very old lady, was doing on the radio. I was playing her granddaughter. Everybody was very nervous about working with the great lady who had some reputation, but none more than a young actor on the Radio Rep – I think he had one line – who was visibly terrified – beside himself with nerves – conscious that he was working with one of the greatest actresses of this century. It was painfully obvious that he wanted to ask the great lady some earth-shattering question. Finally he plucked up the courage. With voice shaking, he stuttered, 'Dame Edith . . . may I . . . ask you something?' She just stared at him with her amazing eagle face in silence. He ploughed on. 'I think you are . . . the greatest actress . . . I have ever*

seen ... you always seem to know how to stress the right word ...'
He paused as he framed the big question. 'How do you know ...
which word to stress?' By this time he was like a plank, he was so
rigid with terror. She stared at him and, after the longest pause I have
ever known, she replied, 'I STRESS THEM ALL.'

Angela Pleasence (actor)

Education

The BBC's Education Directorate is responsible for School Radio and
Adult Education. Although they generally cast from the Radio
Drama Company or actors known to them, they will audition very
occasionally for specific and specialist parts, and listen to demo-
tapes. A demo-tape that shows an awareness of the Education
Department's style of programming will be more suitable than your
commercial demo, so a children's story or rhyme would be apposite.
Listen to the programmes for ideas. Send your demo-tape and CV to
School Radio, Room No. 740, BBC, Broadcasting House, Langham
Place, London W1A 1AA. A standard reply will be sent but your tape
will be circulated to all producers.

BBC English

BBC English makes English-teaching programmes for the World
Service at Bush House. It has its own repertory company (the BBC
English Repertory Company – the 'Rep') which consists of four
actors – two men and two women. Applicants should have a demo-
tape tailor-made but it need not be professionally recorded. It should
be no longer than six minutes and present two or three pieces, one of
which should be straight narrative. A paragraph from a novel or
newspaper would be ideal. Accurate accents are a bonus but the bulk
of the work is 'straight talk' as the World Service is mainly seeking a
range of voices with clear enunciation to present 'the English voice
abroad' in everything from 'pop' to news programmes. They don't
advertise Rep vacancies, relying on word of mouth within the
profession and submitted demo-tapes from which suitable candidates will be invited to audition. Demos are also used to identify
specific voice types that might be required.

The Rep offers a three-month contract, renewable up to eighteen months, so vacancies are intermittent. Send your CV and demo-tape to BBC English, BBC World Service, Bush House, The Strand, London WC2B 4PH.

> *When I was very young I remember holding auditions with a senior producer at the BBC who liked to have the blind down between the control room and the studio. Now I always like to watch people when they are auditioning for radio ... you can tell a certain amount from an actor's stance and movement, and approach to the microphone. Anyway, on this occasion the secretary showed the actor who was due to audition into the studio and we couldn't see him ... but we could hear him scuffling and shuffling his script, and making peculiar noises. We asked if he was ready. 'Be with you in a minute,' he muttered. More shuffling and scuffling. This went on for what seemed an unconscionably long time, so I was dispatched to go in and see what was going on. There was this poor fellow at the table putting full make-up on! He'd even put a wig on! I was flabbergasted 'But this is for radio ...' I gasped. 'I know,' he said, 'but I find it helps.'*
> John Tydeman (former head of BBC Radio Drama)

Voice-overs

Pick up headphones in the Natural History museum and the chances are you will hear a voice talking about molluscs or the ungentle-manly behaviour of the Tyrannosaurus rex. Listen to the voice in the department store lift preaching of riches in Haberdashery or on the PA system reminding you of special offers; the voice in the Underground warning you to 'Mind the Gap' (legend has it that he still gets repeat fees!); the voice backing the promotional film at the Boat Show, the Motor Show, the Ideal Homes Exhibition; the air hostess explaining how to blow up your lifebelt on the video; the voice of British Telecom – all of them are actors! There's an awful lot of work in the voice-over field, such as:

- background narration in TV commercials
- commercials for radio
- commentaries for training films and documentaries, etc.
- cartoon voices
- novels and other books on cassette for the commercial market
- talking books and other products for the blind
- talking newspapers
- dubbed dialogue in foreign films
- CD-ROM.

The first step towards working in voice-overs is to make your demo-tape (see chapter 2). Your first port of call should be the agents who specialise in voice-over work. The *Spotlight* office will give you an up-to-date list. If a voice-over agent takes you on, you will have made a good start. He will do a lot of the legwork and bear much of the expense. He will want a batch of demos (about six) for immediate use. Demos are likely to be biked to clients on request and are rarely returned, so you will need to supply more at regular intervals. If you don't succeed in getting an agent you must be extremely energetic yourself. You need to target:

1 Television and video production companies who dub foreign films into English or make cartoons. A list of production companies currently active in financing and/or making audio-visual products in the UK and international media markets can be found in *The BFI Film and Television Handbook* published by the British Film Institute (21 Stephen Street, London W1 TLN Tel: 020 7255 1444) at £20. This details the kind of work each company undertakes. Work spans the media spectrum from TV commercials and animation series to documentaries and feature films. There is also a list of film, TV and video production companies in *Contacts*.
2 Independent local radio stations (listed in *Contacts*).
3 Book publishers and recording companies who publish books on cassette or CD-ROM. Retail Entertainments Data (020 7566 8216) publishes a Spoken Word Catalogue which lists manufacturing and distributing companies of compact discs, cassettes of spoken

word and miscellaneous recordings (language courses, educational tapes, documentary and instructional recordings, etc.) generally obtainable through record dealers and bookshops in the UK. It is the most comprehensive reference on spoken-word releases in the UK, providing details of over 14,000 currently available titles.

Many recording companies only use star performers, but research will lead you to those that use unknowns. Companies like Chivers and Soundings are two that come to mind.

4 Organisations that cater for the needs of the sight-impaired. The Royal National Institute for the Blind (020 7388 1266) would be a place to start. Talking Books, including everything from James Bond to the Bible, are recorded at the RNIB studios in Great Portland Street. They do hold auditions from time to time. They try to match voices to books, so will audition when they need a specific accent or to fill a gap in their panel of narrators.

Check whether an organisation accepts demo-tapes before dispatching your package. Ask for the name of the person and the department to whom it should be sent. Keep records of where tapes are sent and what response they receive. Ring regularly to enquire about work.

Voice agencies and some advertising agencies (listed in *Contacts*) keep demo-tapes in voice-banks, storing a full range of voices. These fall into various categories, which might typically include the following:

- *Male and female. Voices that cover the age spectrum, deeper voices and high voices.*
- *Quality voices – good, well-spoken English for what is described as 'a nice gentle sell'.*
- *Mimics – artists who can imitate Donald Duck, Prince Charles and the tannoy at City Airport.*
- *'Spotty' voices – adolescent voices to sell teenage products.*
- *Foreign voices and genuine regional accents.*

Think carefully about which category you fall into. Obviously the precise manner in which voices are 'banked' will vary from agency to agency. It would be useful to label your demo with a general voice type to aid classification.

Voice-over artists must be 'on call' and available at very short notice. You or your agent may get a call at 10 a.m. for a job that very afternoon, or, at the latest, the following day, so it is imperative you can be contacted wherever you are. You would be well advised to get a mobile phone or a pager, but failing that, regular calls to check your ansaphone are essential. You must be available to give the client what he wants, when he wants it. The successful artists in the industry can be doing five or six jobs a day. They will not be famous to the general public, but they are much sought after in their field and their income reflects this!

It is important for artists to be businesslike in their approach to this work. Be punctual. Studios are expensive. Girls should remember to be smart. Ad agencies' clients deal in non-bag-lady types! No attitude please – 'I'm an actor first' type of thing. Voice agenting is different from theatrical agenting. It is a lottery. Not the best performers but the available and most businesslike get the work! There is no plan. All is whim. Keep nodding and smiling. We are in the world of commerce, NOT ART.

Stephen Chase (the Rhubarb agency)

7 Some Alternative Markets

Actors have skills to do with their personalities, their voices, their creativity and their presentation. I think actors should be selling their services wherever they can – they shouldn't be 'sniffy' about what people are buying from them. It's very short-sighted for actors to close their minds to any opportunity in these difficult times.

Mo Heard (former Actors' Company Manager, MOMI)

Work for many actors in the conventional marketplace is either intermittent, short-term, temporary or seasonal. The competitive nature of the market in a profession that is acknowledged to be 'overcrowded' means that even experienced performers suffer lengthy periods of unemployment. Nevertheless, if you are prepared to think laterally, be flexible or create your own work, you will find opportunities in some unexpected places.

Here are a few suggestions.

The Platform Performance, Festival and Lecture Circuit

I have received some unlikely requests with regard to my much-travelled one-woman show on the eighteenth-century diarist and novelist Fanny Burney. These include an enthusiastic reply to my standard letter from a university in North America, enclosing a generous contract for my show, Funny Bunny. I signed the contract and sent it back. In due course, not without inner doubts, I went to this university and duly performed my show on Fanny Burney. It was well received, although perhaps a little less warmly, I thought,

than in other venues on the same tour! Had I had an off night? Or
had the university audience, though unwilling to say so, been looking
forward to some light relief and felt let down? Little was said. The
contract was honoured and the money paid. Funny Bunny, *while*
still in its early planning stages, will soon be on vigorous offer to
institutes of higher learning throughout the English-speaking world!

Karin Fernald (actor)

There is a market for small one- or two-person shows about popular
figures of history, literature and romance. You will need to research
and write the show yourself. Such shows have successfully portrayed Fanny Burney, the Brontës, Dylan Thomas, Fanny Kemble
and Canon Rawnsley, who founded the National Trust. The average
length is between fifty and eighty minutes.

Choose a commercial subject and an appealing title. An historical
figure connected with a specific venue might ensure a booking there,
but can you sell it anywhere else? It is just plain foolish to choose a
subject nobody has heard of – unless of course they have heard of
you!

Don't tackle a subject unless you feel really enthusiastic about it. If
you discover an academic who shares your enthusiasm, you might
be able to arrange a performance at his university.

A platform performance can take many forms – anything from a
staged reading with minimal furniture, costume and props to a
dramatised lecture, slide show or a fully-fledged little production. A
platform show should be adaptable enough to be performed
anywhere from a cramped classroom to the Albany Empire. If you
are performing with the text, make sure you are sufficiently familiar
with it to make continual eye contact with your audience. Some
performers feel 'the book' gives added cachet and authority to the
genre. Others feel freer if they learn the text. There seem to be no
hard-and-fast rules and no consistent expectations.

Once your show is written and rehearsed, expend a little 'risk
capital' on hiring a venue to give it a 'test run'. This will give you the
opportunity to see how it works in front of an audience, and smooth
out its flaws. Run off some cheap leaflets on a word processor and

invite along family and friends. The promise of a free glass of wine might even encourage the local press to come along and review it.

You are unlikely to attract bookings until you have established some sort of a track record. Offer free performances to local charities, churches and schools, so you can add them to your list of 'gigs'. Venues that might book your show will include museums, libraries, church halls, bookshops, City Livery Clubs, ladies' luncheon clubs, historic houses, festivals, stately homes and schools. Initially a well-targeted blitz by telephone is far more effective than an expensive mail shot that is likely to get binned. When you ring, make sure you get the name of the person responsible for bookings, so that all subsequent communications will have a personal touch. Follow up with your publicity pack.

You can create an effective document at minimal cost on your computer. Use a loose-leaf format so that you can easily update your pack with information about bookings and reviews. The pack should include:

- An eye-catching title page with the name of your show and the performers
- Contact addresses and telephone numbers, fax numbers, mobile numbers, e-mail numbers and website address – if you have one
- A synopsis of the show and further information about the subject matter
- A list of venues where the show has previously played
- Reviews
- Photographs and biographies of the performers
- A 10 x 8 still from the show
- Your fee
- Any technical requirements with regard to staging, furniture, lighting and sound (i.e. 'All we need is a small table, two chairs, a well-lit playing area and a well-tuned piano or accessible electric point to plug in an electronic keyboard').

Remember that most theatre venues you visit will not be able to provide the manpower to operate complicated sound and lighting plots. Unless you are prepared to travel with your own stage manager and equipment you are bound to hit difficulties. If you are working in a theatre, which offers some technical assistance, send a script ahead of you with clearly marked lighting states, timings and cues. Don't be too ambitious. Four very basis lighting states: (1) a broad, bright general wash, (2) a cross-fade to stage right, (3) a cross-fade to stage left and (4) a downstage centre special 'spot', with the possible addition of a 'special' like a stained-glass window or a moonlight effect, are the absolute maximum you should plan for.

Consider carefully before incurring the added expense of transporting heavy items of furniture. Costumes and small props, on the other hand, give the event a real sense of occasion and can easily be transported in a suitcase on the train or the back of a car. Be prepared to improvise with furniture you find at the venue or, if you have particular requirements, make sure you let the venue know in good time so that they can beg, borrow and steal on your behalf.

> *For one of our shows,* Shakespeare in the Saddle, *I specify for one of the items of furniture either a theatre skip or a bench or a trunk or a low table, the most important thing being that two people can sit safely on it side by side. I list the items in order of preference. I find, if you are flexible, people will generally go to a great deal of trouble to get you exactly what you want.*
>
> Bill Homewood (actor)

Make full use of steps, existing entrances and rostra. Avail yourself of any opportunity to rehearse in the venue beforehand. Be prepared to adapt your show to the space. You may find a wall where you had rehearsed your up-left exit!

Before accepting a booking at any venue, check they have some mechanism for publicising your event. Performing to the Chairperson of the local Association of Knife Grinders and Haberdashers and her mother in a draughty scout hut on the outskirts of Birmingham will be very demoralising!

In most circumstances you will receive a flat fee for your show. Start off by asking around £100 a gig. As your show gains a reputation, you can ask for between £200 and £300, but bear in mind this figure doesn't leave you with a lot of spare change if you have to cover travel, meals and accommodation in the Western Isles. Some venues might offer to split the box-office takings with you. Read the small print in your contract carefully. If you have contracted to pay the salaries of box-office and bar staff out of your share you could end up badly out of pocket. Cancellation is understandably frowned upon, but if you organise Sunday performances, these can usually be fitted round other things.

There are a few agents who handle this kind of work on what might loosely be described as the 'Lecture Circuit'. *Spotlight* will supply you with a list. It is unlikely, though, that they will be significantly more effective than you can be yourself. Capitalise and build on each success until you have a respectable dossier of venues and reviews. Wherever you play, ask the organisers for more suggestions and ideas for gigs in their area.

The great advantage of having your own show is that you are in charge of your own destiny. It is a challenging and rewarding way of 'keeping your hand in'. Some actors have got agents through such work. Some use contracts with venues as contributions towards qualification for Equity membership (see chapter 8). You will need to prove that you have been engaged on at least eight separate occasions for which you have been paid an appropriate professional fee. Equity has no agreement on rates of pay for this kind of work. Check with the union which contracts might be eligible for membership.

The platform performance is not a route to fame and fortune. You are more likely to get a glowing letter from the local Women's Institute than a review in the *Guardian*, but it does offer useful experience to the actor starting out. Indeed, there are many performers who find this kind of work so satisfying that they choose it above everything else. Seasoned practitioners can command £1000 or more a show and appear not only in the UK, but also in Europe and the USA. These shows are as diverse as they are entertaining. Honor Blackman, for instance, has a risqué little show called *Dishonourable Ladies* which charts the history of the femme fatale, while Edward Fox unforgettably performs T. S. Eliot's *Four Quartets*!

The British Performing Arts Year Book is a comprehensive guide to venues, festivals, arts centres and supporting organisations in Britain and Ireland. It is published by Rhinegold Publishing Ltd (020 7333 1700) and updated annually. You will find the *Museums Year Book* (published by the Museums Association Tel: 020 7250 1836) is useful too. This contains detailed information on over 3000 museums, galleries and cultural organisations plus some historic houses. This directory is expensive (£35 to Museum Association members and £100 to non-members) but you'll find it in any good reference library. Private and public schools also have funds to spend on extramural activities and regularly buy in small shows, readings and recitals, especially if they have some bearing on the syllabus. *The Independent Schools Yearbook* (A. & C. Black) will give you a list.

If you want to take your show overseas, talk to the British Council (Tel: 020 7930 8466 or visit their website on www.britishcouncil.org/arts or http://theatredance.britishcouncil.org) where you will find a list of useful publications such as the *Performing Arts Yearbook for Europe* and other helpful information.

Other useful organisations are:

International Intelligence in Culture

4 Badan Place
Crosby Row
London SE1 1YW
Tel: 020 7403 6454
Fax: 020 7403 2009
website: www.intelCULTURE.org

This is an independent agency providing information on funding opportunities available for overseas visits and projects, and also providing contact details for ministries of culture, arts councils and arts organizations across the globe.

EUCLID International

website: www.euclid.co.uk

Euclid is the official UK cultural contact point and provides information on funding and country contacts, network details, publications listings, events listings and latest news.

The Arts Council (Tel: 020 7333 0100) also publish a handbook, *On the road . . . the start-up guide to touring the arts in Europe,* compiled by Ruth Aldridge and Rod Fisher.

Lastly, if you are using any material in your show that is in copyright, remember that performed works are liable for royalty payment if the author has been dead for less than seventy years. Copyright law is complex, so check the availability of rights and royalty requirements before proceeding; you could be obliged to pay a fee to the copyright holders.

Theatre in Education

> *Definitions are a minefield – there is TIE (Theatre in Education), YPT (Young People's Theatre), DIE (Drama in Education), TYP (Theatre for Young People), THE (Theatre in Health Education) – over the last eight years there has been an explosion in TIE exploring health issues (drugs, bullying, HIV/AIDS, etc.) mainly as a result of funding being available in these fields. Then there's Youth Theatre and Children's Theatre, all of which cover distinct areas of work. It's not surprising that the distinctions are now becoming blurred!*
>
> Peter Wynne-Willson (actor, director)

Some actors are dismissive of Theatre in Education (TIE) work, seeing it as a poor relation to the commercial theatre and not sufficiently mainstream for their talents. Yet it is actually a well-rooted professional activity which began life at the Belgrade Theatre, Coventry in the 1960s and is indebted to the work of August Boal (Theatre of the Oppressed) and Joan Littlewood's interactive work with the community at Stratford East.

Although the landscape has altered and many of the traditional TIE companies have gone, or changed beyond recognition, TIE now covers a much wider range of activity than it used to and there are some real new employment opportunities for actors. As theatre budgets are cut and audiences decline, companies are looking at new ways to supplement their incomes. TIE is a rapidly expanding area, which you should consider if you have theatrical skills you feel you can successful transmit to others. Work includes:

* Workshops which use improvisation and storytelling to explore social issues
* Workshops to accompany main-house productions
* Packages for schools exploring set texts
* Short residencies in schools to assist in creating theatrical productions
* Workshops in writing, performing or other theatre skills.

As a result of the emphasis now being placed by the Arts Council and local Arts Boards on the creation of education departments in mainstream theatre companies, or the provision of educational workshops relating to companies' work (a company's ongoing funding is often *dependent* on such provision), it is becoming increasingly common for actors to be required to undertake 'theatre education' work as part of their contract. So it could be to your advantage if you are able to express a genuine interest in education work at your audition. This is especially true of the smaller touring companies whose finances are often underpinned by their outreach activities. The education officer or the assistant director in a smaller company will often spearhead the education arm of the company's work and actors in the show might be contracted to lead workshops alongside their performance commitments. These activities might include anything from improvisation and character-building to expositions of the rehearsal process. If demand is heavy, a company might contract in actors with workshop skills to facilitate specific workshops on their behalf. Workshop leaders may be required either to go out and work with groups in the community, or lead sessions between matinées and evening performances.

Workshops can take many forms, ranging from simple question-and-answer sessions about a play and its characters to more complex interactive performances which could, for instance, lead a local group through an improvised storyline with a whole series of optional endings exploring moral and ethical issues.

If you are asked to run a workshop, find out if there are any in-house training procedures in place to help you. Ensure you are adequately briefed about your group and what is required, and that you have adequate time to prepare the content and structure of your session. Running workshops requires intelligence, imagination, patience, stamina and strongly developed interpersonal skills. It is a teaching job as much as an acting job and not an easy option. If you don't feel confident you can transfer your skills effectively, theatre education work is not for you.

On the other hand, running workshops can be well paid, commanding £120-plus a day. Once you have the necessary teaching skills under your belt, they will prove to be a very saleable commodity. When you have more experience you can charge for preparation time as well.

Adverts for theatre education work – reputable companies seeking workshop leaders, youth theatre leaders, actors and directors, etc., for their Education Department – regularly appear in the classified advertisements of *The Stage*, *Arts Management Weekly* and *The Voice*.

If TIE interests you further you might care to investigate the burgeoning world of 'vocational post-sixteen education' like BTech courses in theatre studies or General National Vocational Qualifications (GNVQ Performing Arts). Ask your local education authority for information. These courses are skills-based, so quite a few actors find themselves employed part-time in sixth-form colleges teaching voice training, acting technique, etc. You might see this as a natural progression from similar work in the theatre. Some colleges are amenable to job-shares because actors' input has proved to be so stimulating.

TIE companies hate being regarded as a way into 'the profession', and are justly proud of their value as a profession in their own right. On the other hand, it is true that working with young people can provide a very broad and powerful grounding in important performance skills. In TIE you are spending your days working in role, devising plays through improvisation, hot-seating with audiences, working in difficult performance spaces, playing a wide range of parts to a wide range of highly critical and demanding audiences. All this can be as valuable a basic training for performers as was supplied in the past by weekly Rep.

Peter Wynne-Willson (actor, director)

The National Trust

The National Trust Theatre Administrator
National Trust Theatre Projects
Sutton House
2 and 4 Homerton High Street
London E9 6JQ
Tel: 020 8986 0242
Fax: 020 8985 2343
e-mail: Tshrkv@smpt.ntrust.org.uk
website: www.nt-education.org

The National Trust Theatre is the National Trust's professional Theatre in Education company which tours a variety of projects based on National Trust issues. Performances take place at National Trust properties and other venues such as schools. Theatre in Education is used to develop new audiences, including a variety of community groups and general adult visitors as well as schools. The tours are streunous and demanding, performing in rural and inner-city areas throughout the year. Performances usually take place twice daily with a maximum audience of fifty. The projects are frequently company-devised with a highly interactive content. The company varies in size from two to five actor/teachers, supported by a full-time administrator and a freelance artistic team.

Actor/teachers who have research and improvisational skills, experience in Theatre in Education work, touring experience and excellent communication skills are favoured. The National Trust advertises in *The Stage*, *PCR* and the Equity Job Service. The company pays Equity minimum on the TMA/Equity contract plus touring allowances.

Information about past and current projects can be found on the Theatre Projects part of their website.

Murder Evenings and Weekends

If you are quick-thinking, witty, with improvisation skills and a lot of nerve, there are an increasing number of 'Murder Mystery' companies that use actors for party events. Several advertise in *The Stage*, others in *The Corporate Entertainment Directory* (cost £30) published by the Nash Corporation, 322 Kensal Road, London NW10 5BZ Tel: 020 8969 2232 and/or on their website at www.corporateentertainment.com

The clients of these organisations are diverse; clients of one company called The Murder Squad, for instance, include large local hotels, British Airways, parent–teacher associations and private individuals celebrating anniversaries and birthdays. They perform their various 'bumpings-off' in venues as diverse as a tent in a Hampstead garden and the *Flying Scotsman*. The company provides a full-time living for nine people, dispatching two teams of actors to perform two shows nightly.

Actors interested in this work should have a sense of humour, be presentable and prepared to travel and perform with minimum rehearsal. You will need to ad lib with party-goers unravelling such mysteries as 'Murder by Auction' or 'Dying for Christmas' and generally enter into the spirit of the occasion. Bright, attractive, 'fun' young women and 'evil-looking' gangster-type young men are favoured!

Christmas is the busiest time, but the more established companies are booked up for most of the year. This is not art but it *is* 'theatre', providing in its way an enjoyable opportunity to keep your skills honed and your brain alive while you wait for more mainstream work to materialise.

There is usually no money for rehearsals but actors can expect a fee of something in the region of £45 per performance, although some companies pay a good deal more. Actors often enjoy free slap-up meals and drinks for the evening. If events are far from home, accommodation is generally provided by the client.

Here are a few companies to be going on with:

Murder Mystery and Mayhem	Tel: 020 8959 6579
Murder Company	Tel: 01484 648673
Murder on the Menu	Tel: 0122 734816
Murder Mystery Dinner Theatre	Tel: 020 7404 4232

I worked for two Murder Mystery companies. For one there was a storyline, but no script – it was improvisation-based and extremely difficult and challenging. You just had to make it up as you went along! The other company worked from a script. I had to learn a huge part in a three-act script, which was invaluable experience. You have an audience, quite a large audience sometimes, people who are eating and drinking and making merry. To learn to engage and hold their attention is a great discipline in itself. Anything else is easy after that! I was lucky to be working with other actors, all of whom were highly talented. I had been to university, not drama school, so it gave me a lot of confidence as a performer. It was good fun and wasn't badly paid either!

Hariet Lake (actor, singer)

Cruise Ships

The cruise industry has expanded enormously over the last ten years. For entertainers and musicians it offers the opportunity to work at a high professional standard, at a good wage in a variety of productions. Rather than perform the same show eight times a week, performers will appear in two or three different shows in a week, often with days off in between. While doing this they can probably save a significant amount of money over the course of a six-month contract and all the time are visiting some of the most beautiful ports in the world.

Tony Rex (Music Director, Openwide International)

There is a lot of work for performers with musical-theatre backgrounds on cruise ships. Review shows and potted versions of West End musicals like *Phantom of the Opera, Miss Saigon, Grease, Me and My Girl* are presented to excellent standards. Some cruise lines like P&O develop shows in-house, but many rely on creative agencies like Openwide International, Tel: 020 8962 3416 – who, along with other creative agencies, sometimes advertise in the back of *The Stage* – to develop and mount their entertainments for them. You might be expected to do four different shows a week but the rest of the time you can enjoy just being 'on board'. Wages are good compared with those of landlubbers, especially as there are many perks including free food, accommodation and many discounted services on board like hairdressing. Creative agencies also advertise for vocalists (your Shirley Bassey imitation would go down a storm), jugglers, speciality acts, music-hall acts, comics, cabaret artists – anything to keep passengers happy on the voyage. The downside is you will be out of town for longish periods and miss auditions. The plus side? Sailing between Florida and the Caribbean islands for six months. Horrid! And you end up with enough money in the bank to avoid the dreaded day job for a while when you get home.

Lookalikes

Look Alikes Ltd
17–23 Lorn Road
London SW9 OAB
Tel: 020 7274 0666
Fax: 020 7274 4466
e-mail: info@lookalikes.ltd.uk
website: www.lookalikes.ltd.uk

If you look like and can impersonate a famous person, being a lookalike could be a lucrative little sideline – especially if you look like someone fashionable like 'Posh' or 'Becks' or an enduring icon like Marilyn Monroe. But it's not enough to look like Tammy Wynette or Eartha Kitt – you have to talk and sing like them as well! You have to be able to mimic your character in every way. 'Marilyn' might be asked to sing 'Happy Birthday' and mingle with the guests at a corporate party, 'The Queen' to officiate at an award ceremony or 'press flesh' at a celebrity function. You might be expected to sustain your character for two or three hours at a time, so you need to be an excellent mimic, to have a sharp wit, stamina and considerable improvisation skills. Lookalikes are often required for TV, films, commercials and advertising as well. £350 plus expenses would not be an unusual fee for an hour of 'Marilyn's' time at a corporate function. You'll probably get a good meal out of it too!

Museum or Gallery Drama

Over the last twenty years, art galleries, museums and stately homes have increasingly seen the value of using actors, drama and interpretative techniques to attract visitors to their doors and 'switch them on' to artefacts, paintings, science, technology, medicine, historical figures and events. The approach was pioneered at the Museum of Minnesota in the USA in the early 1970s, which used character cameos as an effective and popular way of interpreting some of its exhibits. In the UK about a third of all museums now use actors for some kind of historical first- or third-person interpretation, so opportunities for actors to entertain and educate are expanding all the time.

Many ways have been found of implementing gallery drama. In their daily programme of events, some museums present several short (ten-minute) small-scale monologues or dialogues, while others choose to give fewer, comparatively long (thirty-to-forty-minute) presentations involving several actors or even entire companies. Some institutions encourage audiences to keep their distance, whereas others strive for close involvement between visitors and performers. Some adopt an informal approach to the preparation of the actors' pieces (many of which are extemporised round a well-researched brief), others use carefully prepared scripts from which deviation is discouraged. The topics sometimes concern individual exhibits, but they often relate to a whole gallery or even to the entire museum.

Dr Graham Farmelo (Head of Exhibitions, Science Museum)

The Science Museum has led the way in the UK in a field variously known as heritage re-enactment, first-person interpretation, historical interpretation, museum or gallery drama and theatre-in-museum work. What began in the 1980s with a single actor has now become a daily drama programme provided by a company of about thirty actors performing a variety of roles around the museum. Actors are recruited through a specialist company (Spectrum Drama and Theatre Projects) resident in the Science Museum building, which is subcontracted to script and mount interpretative on-site drama events. Actors are often required to write their own scripts with the advice of curators or other experts. The company also subcontracts for a range of other organisations like the Natural History Museum, the National Maritime Museum, the Tate Gallery, the London Transport Museum, Museum of London, Imperial War Museum and HMS *Belfast*.

English Heritage is a huge employer of re-enactors and first-person interpreters too. It runs between 400 and 600 events on around 400 English Heritage sites every year. Events range from battles and displays to historical entertainments in stately homes and ruined castles aimed at giving visitors a genuine flavour of past times. Similar events are organised in Scotland by Historic Scotland, which runs about 300 events on thirty-five historic sites and Cadw – Welsh Historic Monuments. Allen-Drake Events Management manages about a hundred events a year for Cadw on about twenty-five historic sites.

Specialist companies advertise for actors in *The Stage* and the casting information sheets in the usual way, although many say they recruit from recommendations rather than through the audition process. *The Museums Year Book* (available at your public library) gives a comprehensive list of museums, art galleries and some stately homes across the UK. It is well worth identifying those in your area and finding out the names of one of the many companies, like Spectrum, to whom they subcontract this kind of work. If you are feeling entrepreneurial, you could even talk to the curator of your local art gallery, museum or historic site and suggest creating a character relevant to a specific collection or exhibit. First-person interpretation ('I am Thomas Crapper, the inventor of the flushing lavatory. Let me tell you how my invention came about...') and third-person interpretation ('I am Hermione Jobbing-Theatrical dressed as an eighteenth-century lady of quality who might have lived in this great house') are relatively inexpensive and attractive ways of bringing exhibits and places to life. (A friend has got considerable mileage out of enactments of a medieval healing woman and the first female doctor, Elizabeth Garrett Anderson. She has even performed Elizabeth Garrett Anderson in the operating theatre of the London Hospital!)

Because approaches to this kind of work vary considerably, it will be necessary to research local opportunities thoroughly. Sometimes the work focuses on the building itself and past lives, either real or hypothetical; at other times on the artefacts or exhibits it contains and their historical context. There are no hard-and-fast rules in this evolving field. The Royal Armouries in Leeds, for instance, employs a specialist company of actors with sword-fighting and riding skills. They even have their own tilting yard. Only those between five foot eight and five foot ten in height, weighing ten to eleven stone and wearing size seven to size nine shoes need apply!

Pay varies too. Some organisations use volunteers or 'weekend re-enactors' and only pay expenses. Others, like the Science Museum, employ professionals and pay around £60 per day, which compares very favourably with Equity minimum rates. Actors there can expect to work anything between eight and twenty days a month, so regular 'interpreters' can make a decent basic wage. A few companies employ actors on short-term contracts, but more often actors are self-employed and responsible for their own tax and National Insurance contributions. Several actors to do this work in the daytime and a West End show in the evening! The work is generally flexible and can be organised around other acting commitments. High acting standards are expected alongside research and improvisation skills, flexibility, quick thinking and the ability to entertain, communicate and maintain the interest of the visitors. Special skills like mime, physical theatre skills or the ability to play a musical instrument can often be incorporated into the work. Actors who work in this field regularly tend to develop a number of roles to increase their employability, perhaps playing an ARP warden at the Imperial War Museum one day, a conductor at the Transport Museum on another and a Roman centurion 'at home' in the Museum of London at the weekend!

> *You're acting. You're researching. You're writing. You're improvising. You're pushing back the frontiers of knowledge for young minds. For forty-year-olds. For eighty-year-olds. You're using your voice. You're using your body. You're using all the skills you learned at drama school. I find it very rewarding work.*
>
> Richard Hodder (actor)

Role-play

Multinational corporations, banks, local authorities, hospitals, social services departments, the police, etc. are increasingly realising the value of teaching their staff good communication skills and the usefulness of actors for role-play in training situations.

There are no rules for this kind of work. Every situation is different. Here is a brief for an actor role-playing a patient in a training session for student doctors to illustrate how role-play works.

> You are a forty-year-old man – a teacher. Your wife is in hospital. Breast cancer has been diagnosed. The disease has invaded her liver. The prognosis is not good. You are struggling to cope with three young children at home as well as hold down your job. Your daughter, aged fifteen, is rebelling by staying out all night. The younger children are fractious and missing their mother. Your are having to come to terms with the fact that your wife might die ... You have not been sleeping. You knock on the doctor's door. You enter his surgery. You have come for some sleeping pills.

In the space of a ten-minute videotaped 'consultation' it is the student's task to discover why the pills are necessary. He must watch and interpret the patient's demeanour – his lack of eye contact, his manner, his body language. The patient wants pills because he needs to sleep but by the end of the 'consultation' the student should know a great deal more about the patient's situation than his insomnia and be able to offer appropriate medication, support and advice. He must be sensitive and skilful for he will have no prior information about the patient's life or medical history.

When the mock consultation is over the student receives feedback from his colleagues and the facilitator of the training session. The actor offers constructive insights into how the interview went from his point of view as 'the patient'. A replay of the videotape provides the student with an observable example of good and bad practice.

There are a growing number of agencies who supply actors for this kind of work, but at the time of writing they are not listed in *Contacts* and only one or two are listed in the phone book. Role-plays for Training provides actors for local authorities and big corporations like banks and oil companies. Steps Role-Play does similar work. An unnamed loose association working under the aegis of a paid co-ordinator provides actors for St Mary's Hospital Medical School and the Royal Free Hospital in London. Persistent detective work should unearth others.

Here are a few I have located:

Role-plays for Training
38 Springfield Road
London SE13 6SN
Tel/Fax: 020 8318 3892
website: www.roleplays.co.uk

Steps Role-play
13A Borough High Street
London SE1 9SE
Tel: 020 7403 9000
website: www.stepsroleplay.co.uk

Interact
Southbank House
Black Prince Road
London SE1 7SJ
Tel: 020 8333 1087
e-mail: info@interactroleplay.com
website: www.interactroleplay.com

Role-players
Bow House Business Centre
153–159 Bow Road
London E3 2SE
Tel: 020 8981 3900
e-mail: Rolplayers@aol.com

If you feel you have the right skills, make a start by identifying the large organisations with training programmes for their staff. This will be a hit-and-miss affair as only a small percentage use role-play for training. Training and human resources departments should be your first port of call. Enquire whether they use actors for role-play. Ask for names and addresses of the agencies they employ. At the time of writing there are about 100 agencies operating up and down the country and it's a growing industry! Many are proactive about targeting companies with over 500 employees, so you might get lucky.

While good acting skills are essential, role-play might more properly be described as a teaching job. There are no Academy Awards. Role-play is a low-key, unsung public service, so if it's the 'roar of the greasepaint' you are looking for, it might not be right for you. The ability to give insightful and sensitive feedback is more important to the process than your talent as an actor. Reacting is more important than acting in this situation. Confidence, dedication, self-awareness, imagination, improvisation skills and intelligence are crucial attributes for the successful role-player. You might be asked to assimilate and grasp several pages of complex information, so that you are adequately informed to play your role in the training session.

As yet, this is not a very big field and agencies operating in it are not well-resourced, so it is important to be clear that you have the right skills for the job before wasting their time. You might, as in the scenario cited, find yourself in a training situation with vulnerable individuals like trainee doctors, for whom communication skills are a vital adjunct to clinical knowledge, enabling them to handle delicate real-life situations on a daily basis. Students may be nervous of the process, so the actor's handling of the session might be crucial to its success. Or you might be helping to train high-powered executive employees of a multinational who earn more in a year than the average actor earns in a lifetime!

Agencies working in the corporate field tend to be looking for actors between thirty and fifty to play middle-management roles. Black, Asian and Oriental actors with appropriate skills are keenly sought. Actors with experience of similar organisations and jobs in other fields tend to be favoured. There are no Equity rates for this kind of work. It is not well paid and there is not a great deal of it about. Company training budgets are invariably tight. A two-and-a-half-hour session might net you something in the region of £65, although you can earn anything up to £300 if you work for one of the large corporations. You will often be paid extra for preparation time. Agencies are invoiced by their client and would expect actors to have a Schedule D (self-employed) tax status to simplify payment.

Understudies, Covers and Swings

Understudying is a bit of a double-edged sword. Either you spend hours in the dressing room writing a novel or stitching tapestry while your principal gives her deathless Electra through an epidemic of some horrid flu; or she succumbs and you are thrust into an ill-fitting costume after too little rehearsal – and you're 'on'! (The understudy cast of O'Neill's *Long Day's Journey into Night* had only had a couple of two-and-a-half-hour rehearsal sessions a week, so you have to do a lot of work on your own!)

> *The job of the understudy is a strangely alienating one. You never really feel part of the production. It's a waiting game . . . a game of nerves. It all comes down to a question of attitude. You do the homework any actor would do for a part. You go to the British Library and read everything you can about the playwright. You watch as many rehearsals as you can. You read the script every single day, even after you've learned your lines, so that its dramatic structure and development become and remain an integral part of you. And if hanging around in your dressing room night after night instead of sharing the glory and the 'roar of the greasepaint' starts messing with your ego, remember the old maxim: love the art in yourself, not yourself in the art!*
>
> Stephen Ellery (actor and understudy to Charles Dance
> in *Long Day's Journey into Night*)

An actor's instinct is, of course, to 'make the part his own'. The understudy's conundrum is how to do that, *yet* give a performance that delivers the physical and emotional shape of the play the principal actors have grown used to in rehearsal and developed during the course of the run. Relationships grow as the run continues – blocking shifts and rhythms change, so a good understudy must never take his eye off the ball!

Most West End shows, long-running shows, big tours and some of the large Reps like the Chichester Festival Theatre use understudies. As I write, Martine McCutcheon's understudy has been a huge hit in

My Fair Lady at the National. No one wants to be 'off ', but sometimes it can't be avoided. Managements can't afford to cancel big shows, so understudies are an essential 'fail safe' to protect their 'box'.

Some actors make a career and a very nice living out of understudying. They have no desire for the limelight, enjoy the life and no doubt knit lots of jumpers! For others it presents valuable opportunities – it keeps line-learning muscles in trim; offers the chance to get acquainted with top directors and to watch high-profile actors at work, not to mention all those 'useful contacts' you might meet at the first night party! Furthermore, many big companies like the National have understudy showings so you can invite agents and casting personnel to come along. (Many understudies secretly believe they would be better than their principal – given half a chance. Sometimes they are right!) If you're lucky and impress you might get the chance to play the part for real when they recast.

If you don't want to get typecast as an understudy, don't do it for too long. If you think you are better than your principal, don't do it at all!
Stephen Webber (actor)

Understudies in musicals are called covers or swings. In musicals, everybody needs to be covered. Belting out numbers every night is heavy on the voice, so it is more likely for principals to be 'off ' in musicals than in straight plays. A cover might 'understudy' the lead and have a small part of his or her own. If the lead is sick, all covers will move up a place. Swings cover everyone – there will normally be a male swing and a female swing. There's lots of work out there!

Management often cast covers from people they know; understudy calls will go out to agents via SBS or on one of the 'agents only' Internet services, and sometimes via the casting information sheets – but if this kind of work interests you, you can do your own research. What shows have been running for ever? Who is the casting director? (It took me five minutes to find out that Trevor Jackson – Tel: 020 7637 8866 – was casting director for all the Cameron Mackintosh shows.) How long do the casts' contracts run? (The cast of *Art* changes every three months, for instance – *and* they do regular understudy showings!) Which part might you be right for? When do they recast long-running shows like *Cats*, *The Mousetrap* or *Blood Brothers*? Who is the management? Managements generally cast understudies shortly after they have cast the main characters (although they are often not 'employed' before the end of the rehearsal period). Make informed guesses about what might be required, then write and express your willingness to understudy. Keep on the case. Would you make a good Lady Bracknell? Are you the same age and 'weight' as Charles Dance? These days the trend is to hire acting ASMs as understudies because it's cheaper. If you are prepared to undertake stage management duties too, let it be known.

You might find understudying frustrating if your heart is set on Hedda, but at least there's a regular wage coming in, and once the show is open – apart from understudy rehearsals and matinées – you are free to lunch with your agent, attend auditions and do any other work you can fit in. Better than working at MacDonald's!

Understudies should ask themselves every day, 'Am I ready to go on tonight if I have to?' If the answer is 'no' – they should do more work on the part!

James Brooke (former actor, current agent)

Corporate and Training Videos

Another source of work is in the field of promotional or training videos for large organisations. Many have their own in-house video units. I have researched the Police and the Fire Brigade but there are many other rich seams. Why not investigate social services departments, the Confederation of British Industry, banks, airlines, motor manufacturers, oil companies, trades unions, political parties, the Ambulance Service, the Open University?

A well-shot scene from a corporate or training video can be a useful addition to your showreel.

The police

The need for police videos is so huge that there is even an award for the best examples sponsored jointly by the *Police Review* and JVC Professional Products (manufacturers of professional video equipment). Between 100 to 160 videos are entered for the competition each year by police forces across the country. Most of the forces now have some form of in-house video resource and the larger forces even have their own studios and sophisticated editing facilities. Since the inception of the Police Video Award, the sponsors have noticed a significant increase in the use of professional actors, presenters and voice-over artists, and a noticeable improvement in the standard of the submissions as a result. It has led to the inevitable conclusion that police should concentrate on being police and not on being actors . . .

The work falls into four broad categories:

1 Training videos. Re-creation of accidents. Interview techniques
2 In-force news – video-based magazine programmes
3 Briefings for officers in the field
4 Community Relations. Communicating with the general public.

While the Metropolitan Police appear to have a strict policy of only using casting agencies and casting directories to choose actors, the City Police and other regional forces have a more flexible approach. The City Police Video Unit at the Force Training Centre at Bishopsgate, for instance, has a database of agencies and a number of drama schools which they call upon when they are casting. They are also open to individual applications. Units are looking for actors to play police officers, muggers, rapists, drug addicts, arsonists, victims, etc. Quite a number of regional police video units would welcome hearing from specific 'types' to keep on file. Actors from ethnic minorities are actively sought for videos intended to help forces understand and deal appropriately with cultural differences. The police's in-house producers tend to be looking for broad stereotypes, so this kind of work will not challenge your versatility. But you will receive modest payment and be performing a valuable public service too.

Police video units are generally small and are unlikely to pay high fees or travelling expenses, so it would be as well to target local forces if you want to pursue this kind of work.

The fire brigade

There are sixty-five fire brigades in the UK. Most are underfunded, so programme-making is not a high priority. A number have small video units, which film operational incidents and make debriefing videos for in-house training. They use professionals from time to time. The larger brigades offer the best opportunities for work.

The London Fire Brigade's media resources unit, for example, makes corporate training and promotions programmes, which are distributed within their organisation to a staff of around 8000. It also produces a video magazine called *Watchword*, which appears three times a year, consisting of a compilation of news and human-interest stories about firemen and the brigade. While the London Brigade rarely uses actors for work to camera, they use a considerable number of voice-over artists to present their programmes and like to ring the changes so their products continue to be lively and engaging. They tend to locate actors through agencies or by word of mouth but are keen to receive demo-tapes from voice-over artists of either sex with clear, accurate, authoritative voices. An Oxbridge accent is not obligatory. Demo-tapes should be sent either to the Video Producer for the London Fire Brigade or to the Production Director of the Press and Publications Unit.

The video unit at the Greater Manchester Fire Brigade is becoming a flourishing commercial concern that currently makes about ten corporate and training videos a year. This includes joint ventures with other emergency services like the Ambulance Service or the Police and such things as fire safety training films for industry, nursing homes, hospitals and hotels. Like the London Brigade, they regularly use voice-over artists ('corporate' voices, regional accents) whom they locate through a local voice-over agency, but would welcome demo-tapes from unrepresented artists who are aware of the unit's budgetary constraints and are willing to be flexible. They also use in-vision presenters. At the time of writing the unit has just begun to employ actors for reconstructions. An equal opportunities training film was such a success that the unit proposes to employ more actors on future projects as their commercial operations expand. A biannual forty-minute video magazine programme is also planned which will use actors and voice-over artists on a regular basis. The unit will view actors' showreels and return them if a prepaid Jiffy bag is enclosed. CVs and photographs will also be sympathetically considered.

The National Fire Service Training College Video Unit at Moreton-in-Marsh occasionally employs voice-over artists with very clear enunciation who can be understood overseas. The unit makes internal training videos for new recruits and corporate videos to promote the unique facilities of the college, sometimes undertaking external commissions both in this country and abroad.

The London Fire Brigade Media Resource Unit
The London Fire Brigade HQ
8 Albert Embankment
London SE1 7SD
Tel: 020 7587 4900

Greater Manchester Fire Brigade Training Centre
Video Unit
Thompson Street
New Cross
Manchester M4 5FP
Tel: 0161 834 9182

National Fire Service College
Moreton-in-Marsh
Gloucestershire GL56 ORH
Tel: 01608 650831

The Conference and Exhibition Industry

Actors are used regularly by companies making presentations of new products to the press or to the public. The toy company Hasbro, for example, has hired actors to play Cindy and Superman at the annual Toy Fair. Vauxhall has used actors, dancers and singers to promote road safety and features of a new car on their stand at the Motor Show. They also use celebrities who are already associated with products.

The Earls Court and Olympia Exhibition Centre (Tel: 020 7385 1200 website: www.eco.co.uk) will send you a calendar of events on request of exhibitions that take place in Earls Court with the names and addresses of organisers. *The Exhibition Bulletin* (Tel: 020 8846 2800 website: www.e-bulletin.com), which is published monthly, will give you details about exhibitions further afield.

> *If you are a working actor you are the envy of thousands and thousands of people, whatever the job is. Scunthorpe Rep or a day on* The Bill. *You are a working actor and part of a tiny percentage of the profession. Just make the most of it!*
>
> David Quilter (actor)

Student Films

Involvement on a student film project may not be the most professional experience. You could find yourself on a sixteen-hour shoot in the rain with an inexperienced director and lousy catering. On the other hand, a well-shot sequence playing a tasty character will make a valuable addition to your showreel. Send it to that agent who would take you on like a shot *if only he had seen your work ...*

You are unlikely to receive more than minimum expenses, but the exercise is usually beneficial to both the student film-maker, who learns about the casting process and how to handle actors on set, and the actor, who gains valuable experience of the studio environment, working on location and working under pressure with a film crew. It's an experience hard to come by at many drama schools.

The National Film and Television School in Beaconsfield keeps a register of actors' CVs and photographs in the library for their students to refer to when casting. Actors can be used for anything from lighting and camera exercises, workshops and end-of-term projects to much larger graduation pieces, which might eventually be given wider distribution. Such credits can look impressive under the 'Film and TV' heading on your CV. The National Film and Television School runs a three-year, full-time course. Students are involved in making everything from feature films and TV studio dramas to commercials and documentaries, so a wide variety of actors are needed on an ongoing basis. An actor might initially be invited to participate in a lighting master class, for example, and then recommended to the register on the basis of the quality of his participation. The school does not advertise for actors – they have no shortage of volunteers on file!

Several film and TV schools are listed in *Contacts*, but *Media Courses UK* (published by the British Film Institute) offers a comprehensive, nationwide list of media studies courses and the institutions that run them. It identifies those with a practical film-making element, so a little intelligent persistent research should help you establish which courses use actors, how and when they are recruited and what they might be paid. Pop in and pin your CV and photograph on the students' noticeboard of your local college.

The Comedy Circuit

The Comedy Store has these 'open-mike' spots every Thursday. Two of them in the course of the evening, each one lasting five minutes, which is a remarkably short time if you are going down well and a remarkably long one if you're not. It is the club's savage boast that only two per cent of open-mikers clear the hurdle of audience approval, a figure which makes the tail-gunner's job-span look as secure as an undertaker's.

Alan Franks (the *Times* journalist who, above and beyond the call of duty, braved the Comedy Store's open-mike spot for his paper!)

If you can make people laugh, if you can write fresh and funny material and are up to the challenge of a heckling, intelligent audience, full of lager, who don't suffer fools gladly, you might find stand-up comedy a modest little sideline.

Zen and the Art of Stand-up Comedy by J. Sankey (published by Routledge), *Successful Stand Up Comedy* by Gene Perret (published by Samuel French Trade) and *Stand Up! On being a Comedian* by Oliver Double (published by Methuen) are useful books to read before you start. They can be obtained at Offstage Theatre and Film Bookshop, 37 Chalk Farm Road, Camden, London NW1 (Tel: 020 7485 4996) which offers a mail-order service if you live out of town.

Alternative comedy as we know it began in the summer of 1979 with the opening of the Comedy Store in London's Soho. Early pioneers such as Alexei Sayle and Tony Allen helped shape and develop it. It was a response to the joke-orientated reactionary comedy on television from mainstream comics whom many found offensive. The 'gong show' at the Store (the gong was your cue to 'get off') has gone from strength to strength, nurturing many of our favourite performers like Jo Brand and Eddie Izzard.

A fair proportion of this mould-breaking breed were committed, observant young men and women with 'something to say' and an 'in your face' way of saying it. Their language was rich and they had strong views on everything from beauty without cruelty and the government to gay rights and being a vegetarian.

Since the 1980s the circuit has become slightly more mainstream and regular comedy venues have sprung up in many major cities. *Time Out* has a comprehensive list of venues in London.

The hardest part of doing stand-up is getting started. The easiest way to get started is to do a course. The longest-running and certainly the most famous are held at Jackson's Lane Community Centre, which is situated opposite Highgate tube in north London (Tel: 020 8340 5226). They are aimed at beginners, run weekly for seven weeks and are very reasonably priced. The Actors Centre runs some excellent classes too.

Begin by developing a comic persona – it might be a heightened version of your own personality or a 'character' like Harry Enfield's

'Stavros' or Barrie Humphries's 'Dame Edna Everage' – and writing a 'set' (a five-to-ten-minute script) and trying it out on a few honest and supportive friends.

A growing number of clubs have ten-minute 'open-mike' or 'try-out' spots where you can give your set its first public test run. A few open spots will be worth their weight in gold. Stick to the smaller, kinder venues at first and beware of Friday nights – they tend to be 'lads' nights out'. Sunday audiences are likely to be gentler. Don't even *think* about doing an open spot at the more established clubs like the Comedy Store until you've got at least one paid booking under your belt – unless you have penchant for being eaten alive!

One bloke I know was doing this routine about Star Trek *at the Old Red Rose Club on the Seven Sisters Road. And it just wasn't working at all. One heckler shouted out, 'What the hell is this?' Quick as a flash another heckler replied, 'It's comedy, Jim, but not as we know it!'*

Robert Hitchmough (actor and stand-up comic)

'My advice is lose the jersey, Alan.'

The advice was coming from a friend of mine, a young comic called Owen O'Neill who happens, by some coincidence, to be one of tonight's billed professional acts.

'The jersey?'

'Otherwise you'll get Val Doonican from the hecklers.'

Ah yes, the hecklers. This is the first time I have heard them accorded their proper title. Until this moment they have been euphemised by quaint old terms such as 'audience' and 'crowd'.

Alan Franks (journalist)

One summer evening at the Canal Café in Maida Vale, my two young daughters were in the audience. About twenty minutes into my set, my five-year-old, Kitty, got a bit restless and started to heckle me. Armed with the microphone, I started to put her in her place. She just fired back with a quick reply to everything I said.

'Guess who won't be getting any pocket money this week?'

'You!'

'If you think you're so smart, why don't you come up here and do it . . .'

She was on her feet and on the stage before I could say 'Oh my God!' I handed her the mike and shuffled off to the side of the stage while she confidently told surreal stories about penguins and flies, not a hundred miles away from some of my own material. It took a lot of coaxing to get the mike back, but eventually she left the stage to tumultuous applause, which signalled the arrival on stage of my seven-year-old daughter Lily! She proceeded to tell the joke about the elephant and the mouse walking together through the jungle. It went down a storm.

It was very quiet in the car as we drove back home that evening. The competition had been very tough!

Norman Lovett (actor and comic)

Be analytical. Be ruthless. If your material doesn't work, cut it. Ask the more seasoned comics on the circuit or the proprietor at the club for feedback and advice. Lose the jersey! If laughs don't come where you expected them (or at all!), keep your nerve, rethink, rewrite and rework, then try it out again at as many open spots as you can organise until your set is honed, your timing is perfect and you are confident your act is fit for the road. If your material is topical and sounds as if it really happened – so much the better.

Success in an 'open spot' may lead to a paid ten-minute half-spot. Most spots are twenty minutes, although they can be as long as half an hour, or even forty minutes once you make your name. Word will get around and you may be recommended to other clubs. After that, you're on your own. It's the usual hard task to persuade clubs to book you. Phone calls. Arm-twisting. Persistence. A list of venues where you have performed deathless open spots or half-spots should persuade the small-to-medium-range venues to give you a chance, especially if recommendations have reached their ears. Die the death and you are unlikely to be asked back. And you may not want to be!

Stand-up comedy can be an excellent second string for an actor with appropriate skills. Quite a few who started out on the comedy circuit as a sideline have ended up developing it as successful full-time career. Others have used it as a springboard for more serious theatrical ambitions. It is hard work both in terms of performance, writing and updating your material, but it means you are free during the daytime for auditions, it polishes up performance skills and comedy timing, and – important for actors who might be employed on TV or film – venues are prepared to cancel or reschedule your spot if necessary.

The rate of pay on the circuit is around £30–£80 for a twenty-minute slot at a medium-scale venue. At some venues performers are paid a percentage of the takings.

The people are so close. They are lapping at my feet, with their faces looking up like gargoyles. They are as close as a jacket. I had no idea you could get vertigo from eighteen inches up. I am dying. They have smelled fear and I am dying. They have seen blood and sprouted dorsals. I see what is meant by dying. The life simply drains out of you and you are left there in whatever condition people find themselves in after they have died. It is not painful because it is beyond pain's familiar calibrations. The needle has gone off the dial. You just go posthumous, and the world too goes dead and numb around you like a deep valley in nuclear winter. Nothing except the end of the end, if such a thing exists. Somehow I still manage to hear a sharp, punctuating sound – a hammer in the fog. It comes once and then again and again. The sound is 'Off'. If I can make it to the song . . . heave myself on to the far bank . . . I will be safe there.

Alan Franks (journalist)

* * *

These are just a few of the alternative avenues you can explore. It's by no means a comprehensive list. I hope it will inspire you to find more. What about video games, CD-ROM, non-singing parts in opera, street theatre, stunt work, 'skin' work and body doubling? Keep your eyes peeled and start researching.

Over to you!

8 The Union

Membership of Equity (British Actors' Equity Association) is open to everyone exercising professional skills in the provision of entertainment in the United Kingdom other than instrumental musicians. Not only does the Equity 'card' give you tangible proof of your credentials as a performer, it also confers on you all the fruits of sixty-odd years of union negotiations and the democratic right to participate in its work.

All actors who have received an Equity contract will already have benefited from the terms and conditions of employment and pay scales negotiated by the union, regardless of whether they are union members. Membership also entitles you to a system of additional safeguards, guidelines, advice and services. If, for instances, you fall off the stage in a blackout because there are no working lights or are hurled from a rogue horse on a film set you will have immediate access to Equity's legal advice and protection service. As long as you are covered by Equity the case won't cost you a penny! In 1994–5 Equity's solicitors successfully concluded forty-nine personal injury claims resulting in payments of over £772,000 in compensation paid to members (which excluded a massive pay-out of £650,000 to the family of Roy Kinnear, who was tragically killed on a film set).

Equity also protects your professional name, so no other Equity member is entitled to be called Hermione Jobbing-Theatrical like you! This ensures you receive all payments and plaudits due.

While it is no longer necessary to join the union, there seems no increase in actors' reluctance to do so; nor has the situation changed much since a series of legislative measures introduced in the mid-1980s made it illegal for employers to discriminate against union members or refuse to employ somebody because they are not a member. Little has altered since the legislation, despite fears that it would 'open the floodgates to all and sundry'.

The profession has quite rightly always required 'the relevant amount of professional experience' from job applicants and union membership continues to be one useful benchmark of this for many casting personnel.

The union's ongoing activities include advice and support in relation to pension plans, insurance, tax and welfare benefits; the negotiation of concessionary rates for health insurance; framing health and safety regulations; agreements relating to residuals and equal opportunities; publicising and informing members and agents about the dangers and opportunities of new technology (CD-ROM, video on demand and the digital manipulation of images); protecting performers' rights over their recorded work; campaigns for increased arts funding and sustaining the interests of British actors overseas through Equity's affiliation with the International Federation of Actors.

> *Protecting performers' rights over their recorded work is increasingly the union's most important work. Who, ten years ago, would have predicted that there would be so much cable and satellite TV? Who, five years ago, would have predicted that there would be British actors' work being used on the Internet? Who could now predict what will be happening in five years' time? So increasingly our contracts say 'this specifically excludes any new media that may occur after this contract is signed'.*
>
> Martin Brown (Equity)

In a profession where supply increasingly outstrips demand, with massive unemployment and modest minimum salaries, where opportunities for exploitation are legion, actors need all the support they can get to defend their rights and bargaining strength in the marketplace. In unity is strength. Equity now has over 35,000 members.

If you become a member you will have the right to elect to join your local branch and attend its meetings. Equity branch meetings are arenas for sharing information, initiating projects, forging friendships and seeking support and advice either from other members or guest speakers who regularly speak at meetings and share their expertise. While London and the south-east is better served than the rest of the country for branches, there is a network of branches throughout the country so you should be able to find one within travelling distance. The *Equity Journal* (published quarterly and sent to members) carries details about venues, dates and contact numbers; alternatively, Equity will provide you with a contact sheet on request. The *Journal* also contains news and information about the profession and union activities.

If you are not a member of the union and want to be one, write to the British Actors' Equity Association, Guild House, Upper St Martin's Lane, London WC2H 9EG Tel: 020 7379 6000. They will send you a user-friendly information pack about terms of entry, membership rates (which are staggered to reflect your income) and details about the many services and benefits the union offers.

9 Maintaining your Skills

Having been an actor for some thirty years, it seems to me that we British actors are, for the most part, a pretty lazy lot who don't see the point of putting ourselves out to go to classes once we've left drama school. In America it's a whole different culture. In New York, for example, actors do classes all the time, keeping their skills in trim just like dancers and singers.

Ellis Jones (actor and course director at the
Royal Academy of Dramatic Art)

If you want to get to Carnegie Hall, you really do have to practise!

Don Warrington (actor)

It is difficult to hang on to a sense of identity as an actor if there are few opportunities to work in your chosen profession. The longer you draw state benefits, the longer you slog away at some soul-destroying job, the longer you wait for the next audition, the more your self-esteem will wither on its stem. Most actors have to earn a crust while they are 'resting' and there aren't all that many jobs you can pick up and put down again. You quickly begin to *feel* like a typist, a labourer, a teacher or a cleaner, unless you focus clearly on your objectives as an actor and always see yourself as being 'in training' for the next job.

If you are to continue to develop as an actor, burnishing your craft, marketing your product and raising your professional profile must now be part of your daily routine.

A good actor never rests. Your voice, your body, your intelligence and your imagination are all the tools you have. It is your duty as an artist to maintain and cherish them.

An actor must always be ready to join the creative act at the exact moment determined by the group. In this respect his health, physical condition and all his private affairs cease to be just his own concern. A creative act of such quality flourishes only if nourished by the living organism. Therefore we are obliged to take daily care of our bodies so we are always ready for our tasks. We must not go short of sleep for the sake of private enjoyment and then come to work tired or with a hangover. We must not come unable to concentrate. The rule here is not just one's compulsory presence in the place of work, but physical readiness to create.

Jerzy Grotowski (from *Towards a Poor Theatre*,
published by Methuen)

If you went to a good drama school you will already know some useful voice and breathing exercises. Do a basic voice warm-up for twenty-to-thirty minutes every day. Include exercises to stretch and free all joints and muscles. Work on breathing, resonance and articulation. Your voice is your instrument. It must be varied, relaxed, flexible, expressive, accurate and strong. Care for it as if it were a Stradivarius. Develop its power and its range.

Paul Scofield as the Moor. Nicol Williamson as Iago. Director: 'Paul. Nicol. I'm afraid there's a bit of a problem. You both sound alike.' Paul: 'No problem. I'll go down in the register and "Moor up" the voice a bit more.'

John Tydeman (former head of BBC Radio Drama)

A good voice teacher will spot your strengths and weaknesses, and give you a programme of exercises. A couple of books you will find useful are *Voice and the Actor* by Cicely Berry (Virgin) and *The Right to Speak* by Patsy Rodenburg (Methuen).

Eat good food. Exercise regularly. Keep drinking and smoking to a minimum. Healthy habits will keep your body in good shape, your skin and hair in good condition and your mind alert. Those elderly movie stars are not flat-bellied and muscled by accident! They work out. Your local gym will help you develop a programme of exercises.

Walk instead of taking the bus. Swim. Go biking. Enrol with a cheap aerobics or dance class. (They are usually advertised on noticeboards in the public library.) Being fit will engender a more positive attitude to both life and work.

Read everything you can lay your hands on. Drama, poetry, prose, biography and autobiography. Read newspapers and magazines. Listen to music. Visit exhibitions. Learn a foreign language. Go to the theatre. See the latest movies. Be adventurous. Engage with life – experience provides the nutrients for an actor's imagination. Everything you see, everything you learn, everything you understand will contribute to your interior ripening as an artist.

> *When actors are not working they should read as many plays as they can. That is part of their tradition. I am horrified by the ignorance of the majority of actors about the whole literary canon. When you're not working, read all the plays so you know them. Keep the grey cells going by actually learning roles you may never play. Take your mind for a canter every day. Reading is important. Learning is important. Looking after your body is important. Just as a painter looks at the world in a certain way . . . as a writer does too . . . so an actor should. Study the world. Earwig like crazy. Observe. Observe. An actor is an artist and the raw material of his art is around him all the time.*
>
> John Tydeman (former head of BBC Radio Drama)

Ongoing Training

> *Acting is a complex and demanding craft, which is hard to practise. After drama school there is nowhere for an actor to exercise that craft, to talk about it and develop it apart from the Actors Centre. It is the only building in London dedicated to the most important element in the theatre – the actor. Where would we be without it?*
>
> Tim Pigott-Smith (actor)

At whatever stage you have reached in your career, the more skills you acquire, the more you develop your artistry, the better your chances of survival and success. You can learn a great deal by getting out there and 'doing it' when the opportunities arise, but have you learned to juggle or dance a pavane? How much do you know about theatre history? How many songs are there in your repertoire? When did you last work on your audition pieces? How long since you developed something new? One of the joys of the profession is that you never stop learning.

> *I was doing* The Secret of Sherlock Holmes *by Jeremy Paul in the West End with Jeremy Brett – it ended on a moment in which Holmes picks up a book and starts to read, and Watson strikes a match and lights his pipe. The curtain comes down on this quiet scene. On several occasions we got to the end of the play, I struck the match and it broke, practically setting me on fire – which completely destroyed the moment. After a year's run – on the very last night – after five hundred performances, I opened the box of matches and was able to look at the matches and pick one that I could see was not broken. And I remember thinking very vividly, 'It's taken me a year to arrive at this point.' I had to do it five hundred times before the actor's 'third eye' could obviate a broken match destroying the moment.*
>
> Edward Hardwicke (actor)

The Actors Centre
1A Tower Street
London WC2H 9NP
Tel: 020 7240 3940
Fax: 020 7240 3896
e-mail: act@actorscentre.demon.co.uk

The Actors Centre is the country's only full-time training base for performers in all branches of the entertainment industry. It was founded in 1978 and is now based in the heart of London's West End – offering professional actors a vital and unique opportunity for ongoing training. These are exciting times for the centre. It is currently being refurbished, giving it modern studio facilities, proper access for people with physical disabilities and a fully functioning West End fringe theatre space – a receiving and producing house which will add both opportunity and credibility to the organisation and its growing membership. I cannot recommend the Actors Centre too highly. Training is, in the end, what separates the professional from the amateur.

The centre is open to all Equity members, registered graduates in their first year of registration and foreign actors holding an Equity letter of exemption, so you will be certain to share classes with actors who have reached the minimum professional standard required to get their 'card'. Membership currently costs £40 per year, £25 per six months and entitles you to a wide range of subsidised classes and workshops taken by experienced tutors and directors who work actively in the industry.

> *Joining the Actors Centre was a major turning point for me. I'd always wanted to, but until I had my 'card', I couldn't. Once I got my 'card' I went along and enrolled for classes, and met other actors who helped me get work; they shared information with me, put me in touch with various groups, casting information services and so on, which I followed up with letters, CVs, phone calls, meetings ... If there's anything at all on the Actors Centre noticeboard that interests me, I'm on to it like a shot!*
>
> Hariet Lake (actor and singer)

Daytime and evening classes are structured so that members at every level of experience can identify those classes that accommodate their needs. The centre delivers everything from basic acting courses to in-depth exploration of classical or modern texts. The short courses are organised to give actors the best opportunity to continue to earn a living while at the same time giving a spur to their creativity.

The Actors Centre also has an excellent, cheap Green Room Restaurant where members can chat and eat, and a fully licensed bar.

Members receive a programme of classes every three months, which lists the wide range of tuition on offer, including audition technique, sight-reading, poetry-speaking, improvisation, clowning, tap-dancing, singing, mime, mask and movement work, Alexander Technique as a basis for interpretative expression, dialects and phonetics, text and acting styles, marketing and cutting-edge experimental 'lab' work. The centre prides itself on being up to date about developments in all the aural and visual media.

The schedule offers an incredibly wide spectrum of classes, from the excitingly eclectic to the rigorously practical, all delivered by doyennes and doyens of our profession and a few young Turks as well!
Mark Wing-Davey (actor, director and
Artistic Director of the Actors Centre)

Classes can be booked by post, telephone, in person or by e-mail on bookclass@actorscentre.demon.co.uk Book early to avoid disappointment! As you can imagine, classes with leading theatre and TV directors and top-flight actors are heavily subscribed! The centre receives subsidies from television and theatre companies who recognise the contribution the centre makes to the industry, so classes with actors like Julian Glover or Frances de la Tour will cost about the same as a couple of sandwiches and a cup of tea!

A number of workshops have a performance dimension and dates are usually set aside every quarter for members to show work in progress in the Tristan Bates Theatre – the centre's well-equipped fringe theatre space. These occasions have the advantage of being directed by approved Actors Centre personnel who have both the skills to develop a performer's work and initiate projects which are of interest to a wider audience.

There are also associated centres in Newcastle, Manchester and Glasgow.

Actors Centre North East
1st Floor
1 Black Swan Court
Westgate Road
Newcastle-upon-Tyne NE1 1SG
Tel: 0191 221 0158

The Northern Actors Centre
30 St Margaret's Chambers
5 Newton Street
Manchester M1 1HL
Tel: 0161 236 0041

Scottish Actors Studio
c/o Equity
114 Union Street
Glasgow G1 3QQ
Tel: 07000 229288 and 0141 248 2472
Fax: 0141 248 2473
e-mail: abyatt.sas@virgin.net

The Ciy Literary Institute

The City Lit (City Literary Institute) Drama Department also runs some classes for Equity members or actors with comparable experience. Excellent courses on voice, audition technique, singing and characterisation are available.

The City Lit
16 Stukeley Street
(off Drury Lane)
London WC2B 5JL
Tel: 020 7242 9872

Other courses in the prospectus (published annually, plus a summer supplement) will be of use to professionals seeking to supplement their skills. Classes are offered in stage combat, where actors can work towards the British Academy of Stage and Screen Combat Proficiency tests and there are advanced classes in ballet, tap, clowning, dialect, juggling, etc. The City Lit is government-subsidised so can offer classes at exceptionally cheap rates. All tutors in the Drama Department are members of British Actors' Equity.

RADA

(The Royal Academy of Dramatic Art)
62–4 Gower Street
London WC1E 6ED

RADA runs short courses in the summer. Their Acting Shakespeare course (June/July) caters both for young professional actors and drama graduates from America and other English-speaking colleges. The RADA Summer School (July/August) offers drama workshops on Shakespearean acting and related skills for students, teachers and anyone interested in acting.

RADA also runs one-week refresher courses in summer, winter and spring for professional actors wishing to re-energise their skills. While the summer schools are expensive, the cost of the refresher courses is kept deliberately low so as not to deter serious participants.

The RADA prospectus and brochure about short courses is available on request.

Several other leading drama schools, including Central School of Speech and Drama, LAMDA and the Webber Douglas Academy of Dramatic Art, also offer short courses and summer schools for actors at every stage of their professional development.

> *You need five assets to succeed as an actor: sharp elbows; will power; knowledge of who you are and what you've got to sell; knowledge of the market; and finally, talent.*
> Ellis Jones (Course Director, the Royal Academy of Dramatic Art)

> *Oh, how seldom does anything happen all by itself in the theatre, or in the performance of even the most gifted actor . . . It does happen, but not often. To know how to work, really to make an effort – that takes talent too. Even an enormous talent. Inspiration is born of hard work. It is not the other way round. Professionalism is a very necessary and sound basis for beginning any work, in any field of art . . .*
> *Stanislavski's Legacy* (edited and translated by Elizabeth Reynolds Hapgood, published by Max Reinhardt)

I hope there are two strong messages in this book; firstly, that to achieve your artistic potential requires the ongoing development of your art and craft, whether you are in work or not. Work may sometimes be 'part-time', but acting is a full-time profession! Second, for most actors the opportunities they deserve will only be achieved by a rigorous and intelligent programme of networking and marketing. We can all 'be brilliant in the bedroom' but success is essentially down to your determined effort to develop the quality of your 'product' and sell it in an overcrowded marketplace. I hope these are messages that, in tandem with information and practical advice, will invigorate and inspire your work in this exacting but wonderfully rewarding profession.

> *Never meddle with play-actors, for they're a favoured race.*
> (from *Don Quixote* by Cervantes)

Good luck with it all!

Useful Books

C. Jackson, S. Honey, J. Hillage, J. Stock, *Careers and Training in Dance and Drama* (The Institute of Manpower Studies)

Jean Marlow, *Classical Audition Speeches for Men* (A. & C. Black)

Jean Marlow, *Classical Audition Speeches for Women* (A. & C. Black)

Jean Marlow, *Actors' Audition Speeches for all Ages and Accents* (A. & C. Black)

Jean Marlow, *Actresses' Audition Speeches for all Ages and Accents* (A. & C. Black)

Monologues for Actors of Colour (male), (Routledge)

Monologues for Actors of Colour (female), (Routledge)

Monologues on Black Life (Heinemann)

A Brave and Violent Theatre (Irish monologues), (Smith and Kraus)

James Duke, *How to be a Working Actor* (Virgin)

Simon Dunmore, *The Actor's Guide to Getting Work* (Papermac)

Michael Earley and Phillipa Keil (eds), *The Classical Monologue (Women)*, (Methuen)

Michael Earley and Phillipa Keil (eds), *The Classical Monologue (Men)*, (Methuen)

Michael Earley and Phillipa Keil (eds), *The Modern Monologue (Women)*, (Methuen)

Michael Earley and Phillipa Keil (eds), *The Modern Monologue (Men)*, (Methuen)

Michael Earley and Phillipa Keil (eds), *Women: The Contemporary Monologue* (Methuen)

Anne Harvey (ed.), *The Methuen Audition Book for Young Actors* (Methuen)

Annika Bluhm (ed.), *The Methuen Audition Book for Women* (Methuen)

Brian Bates, *The Way of the Actor* (Century)

Malcolm Taylor, *The Actor and the Camera* (A. & C. Black)

Richard Belzer, *How to be a Stand Up Comic* (Citadel)

Gene Perret, *Successful Stand Up Comedy* (Samuel French Trade)

Tony Jackson (ed.), *Learning Through Theatre – New Perspectives on Theatre in Education* (Routledge)

The Arts in Schools: Principles, Practice and Provision (Calouste Gulbenkian Foundation)

Daniel Dahl, *Drama in Schools* (Arts Council of Great Britain)

K. Winser (ed.), *Arts Professionals in Schools – A Step-by-Step Guide to Artists-in-Schools Projects* (Norfolk Educational Press)

Gerard Nierenberg and Henry Calero, *How to Read a Person Like a Book* (Thorsons, an imprint of HarperCollins)

Nina Finburgh, *Some Dos and Don'ts of Sight-Reading for Actors at Audition* with illustrations by Anne McArthur (Maverick)

ISM Register of Professional and Private Music Teachers (The Incorporated Society of Musicians)

The Singer's Music Theatre Anthology (Hal Leonard Publishing Corporation)

BFI Film and Television Handbook (The British Film Institute)

Media Courses UK (The British Film Institute)

The British Performing Arts Year Book (Rhinegold Publishing Ltd)

Museums Year Book (The Museums Association)

The Independent Schools Yearbook (A. & C. Black)

The Corporate Entertainment Directory (The Nash Corporation)

The White Book (Inside Communications Ltd)

Useful Addresses

Advertising
Spotlight (also **Contacts**)
7 Leicester Place
London WC2H 7BP
Tel: 020 7437 7631
Fax: 020 7437 5881
e-mail: info@spotlightcd.com
website: www.spotlightcd.com

Ugly Enterprises Ltd
Tigris House
256 Edgeware Road
London W2 1DS
Tel: 020 7402 5564
Fax: 020 7420 0507
e-mail: info@ugly.org
website: www.ugly.org.

Bookshops
Offstage Theatre and Film Bookshop
37 Chalk Farm Road
London NW1 8JA
Tel: 020 7485 4996

French's Theatre Bookshop
52 Fitzroy Street
London w1P 6JR
Tel: 020 7387 9373

Casting information providers
The Equity Job Information Service
(Equity Members only)
The British Actors' Equity Association
Guild House
Upper St Martin's Lane
London WC2H 9EG
Tel: 020 7379 6000

PCR (Production and Casting Report)
PO Box 11
London N1 7JZ
Tel: 020 7566 8282
Fax: 020 7566 8284
website: www.pcrnewsletter.com

***ACID* (Actors' Casting Information Department)**
Acid Publications
Suite 247
27 Store Street
London WC1E 7BS
Tel/Fax: 07050 205 206
e-mail: ACIDnews@aol.com

Castcall
106 Wilsden Avenue
Luton LU1 5HR
Tel: 01582 456213
Fax: 01582 480736
e-mail: admin@castcall.co.uk
website: http//www.castcall.co.uk

Cast-Net
99 Windmill Lane
Bushey Heath
Herts WD2 1NE
Tel/Fax: 020 8420 4209
e-mail: Cast_Net@hotmail.com
website: www.castnet.co.uk

DannyRose.com
Avonmouth House
6 Avonmouth Street
London SE1 6NX
Tel: 020 7407 2123
Fax: 020 7357 8063
Mob: 07967 330 853
e-mail: charlied@dannyrose.com
website: www.dannyrose.com

e-media-c
95–96 New Bond Street
London W1S 1DB
Tel: 020 7518 1340
Fax: 020 7518 1341
e-mail: info@e-media-c.net
website: www.e-media-c.net

Demo-tapes

Stephen Chase
Rhubarb Productions
9–15 Neal Street
Covent Garden
London WC2H 9PW
Tel: 020 7836 1336

Bernard Shaw
Horton Manor
Canterbury CT4 7LG
Tel: 0122 773 0843
e-mail: Bernardshaw@talk21.com
website: www.bernardshaw.co.uk

Stanley Productions
147 Wardour Street
London W1V 3TB
Tel: 020 7439 0311

East London Cassettes and Ideal Mastering
65–69 East Road
London N1 6AH
Tel: 020 7251 6630

The Heritage Industry
(England)
Head of Special Events
English Heritage
429 Oxford Street
London W1R 2HD
Tel: 020 7973 3000

(Scotland)
The Events Manager
Historic Scotland
Longmore House
Salisbury Place
Edinburgh EH9 1SH
Tel: 0131 668 8835

(Wales)
Cadw – Welsh Historic Monuments
Allen-Drake Event Management
The Alley
Cosheston
Pembroke Dock
Swansea SA72 4TY
Tel: 01646 685552

The National Trust
National Trust Theatre Projects
Sutton House
2 and 4 Homerton High Street
London E9 6JQ
Tel: 020 8986 0242
Fax: 020 8985 2343
e-mail: Tshrkv@smpt.ntrust.org.uk
website: www.nt-education.org

Overseas Contacts
The British Council
10 Spring Gardens
London SW1A 2BN
Tel: 020 7930 8466
website: www.britishcouncil.org/arts
or http://theatredance.britishcouncil.org

International Intelligence in Culture
4 Badan Place
Crosby Row
London SE1 1YW
Tel: 020 7403 6454
Fax: 020 7403 2009
website: www.intelCULTURE.org

EUCLID international
website: www.euclid.co.uk

Photographs
Image
56 Shepherds Bush Road
London w6 7PH
Tel: 020 7602 1190
Fax: 020 7602 6219
website: www.imagephotographic.com

Courtwood Profiles
Courtwood
Freepost TO55
Penzance TR18 2BR
Tel: 01736 365 222
Fax: 01736 350 203

Setting up a co-op
ICOM
(the Industrial Common Ownership Movement)
74 Kirkgate
Leeds LS2 7DJ
Tel: 0113 246 1737
Fax: 0113 244 0002

Showreels
The Video Casting Directory Ltd
1 Triangle House
2 Broomfield Road
London sw18 4HX
Tel: 020 8874 3314

the plain vanilla company
57 Purdy Street
London E1 3PD
Tel: 020 7515 4865

Quilter-Stott Productions
22 Sherlock Court
Dorman Way
London NW8 0RU
Tel: 07973 222 407

Stand-up comedy
Jackson's Lane Community Centre
269A Archway Road
London N6 5AA
Tel: 020 8340 5226
Fax: 020 8348 2424
e-mail: jacksonslane@pop3.poptel.org.uk

Training
The Conference of Drama Schools
The Secretary
1 Stanley Avenue
Thorpe
Norwich NR7 0BE
Tel/Fax: 01603 702021
e-mail: enquiries@cds.drama.ac.uk
website: www.drama.ac.uk
(The professional association representing leading drama schools in
the UK)

The Actors Centre
1A Tower Street
London WC2H 9NP
Tel: 020 7240 3940
Fax: 020 7240 3896
e-mail: act@actorcentre.demon.co.uk

Actors Centre North East
1st Floor
1 Black Swan Court
Westgate Road
Newcastle-upon-Tyne NE1 1SG
Tel: 0191 221 0158

The Northern Actors Centre
30 St Margaret's Chambers
5 Newton Street
Manchester M1 1HL
Tel: 0161 236 0041

Scottish Actors Studio
c/o Equity
114 Union Street
Glasgow G1 3QQ
Tel: 07000 229288 and 0141 248 2472
Fax: 0141 248 2473
e-mail: abyatt.sas@virgin.net

The City Literary Institute
(The City Lit)
16 Stukeley Street
(off Drury Lane)
London WC2B 5JL
Tel: 020 7242 9872

RADA
(The Royal Academy of Dramatic Art)
62–4 Gower Street
London WC1E 6ED
Tel: 020 7636 7076
Fax: 020 7323 3865

The Central School of Speech and Drama
Embassy Theatre
64 Elton Avenue
London NW3 3HY
Tel: 020 7722 8183

LAMDA
Tower House
226 Cromwell Road
London SW5 0SR
Tel: 020 7373 9883
Fax: 020 7370 4739

Webber Douglas Academy of Dramatic Art
30 Clareville Street
London SW7 5AP
Tel: 020 7370 4154
Fax: 020 7373 5639

The Union
The British Actors' Equity Association
Guild House
Upper St Martin's Lane
London WC2H 9EG
Tel: 020 7379 6000

The Director's Guild of Great Britain
Acorn House
314–20 Grays Inn Road
London WC1X 8DB
Tel: 020 7278 4343

Index